Mothering for the State

Mothering for the State

The Paradox of Fostering

Baukje (Bo) Miedema

Fernwood Publishing • Halifax

Editing: Brenda Conroy
Cover illustration: Neils and Aroon Thakker
Design and production: Beverley Rach
Printed and bound in Canada by: Hignell Printing Limited

A publication of:
Fernwood Publishing
Box 9409, Station A
Halifax, Nova Scotia
B3K 5S3

Fernwood Publishing Company Limited gratefully acknowledges the financial support of the Ministry of Canadian Heritage and the Canada Council for the Arts for our publishing program.

Canadian Cataloguing in Publication Data

Miedema, Baukje.

Mothering for the state

     Includes bibliographical references.
     ISBN 1-55266-010-9

1. Foster mothers -- Canada. Foster home care -- Canada. I. Title.

HQ759.7M52 1999   362.733   C99-950008-2

Contents

List of Tables in Appendix

For my loving family:

Dirk, Sjoerdje, Aaltje, Ajit, Aroon and Niels

Preface and Acknowledgements

My sons were the initial inspiration to examine foster care. I once wondered what would happen if, for whatever reason, both my husband and I were not able to look after our children. Somebody suggested that they would likely be placed in foster care. Having little knowledge about foster care, I became intrigued and wanted to know more. The project was born. Foster care, I have learned, is very closely related to mother care— women are the dominant caregivers and the care they provide is twenty-four hours a day. However, foster care and mother care are seldom discussed simultaneously. I believe that, in order to understand foster-care mothers, one needs to understand mothering.

Mothering is the most rewarding and the most difficult activity one can imagine; it is all consuming and overpowering. All human emotions, good and bad, are amplified in the activity of mothering. Mothering can create the most tender moments in one's life but it can also provide the most painful ones. Mothering is a collective activity—billions of women are mothers; yet it is very personal and private. Mothering is rooted in the past but it is also separate from the past. For example, I have adopted some of the mothering style of my mother; yet I have not duplicated it entirely. I am quite a different mother than she is. The reasons for this are simple, yet complex. I mother in a different time. My mother was poor and motherless by the age of eleven. She had to quit school (she still regrets that) so she and her older sister could care for the other children in the family. I never had such concerns and grew up carefree and able to get the education I wanted.

This book is not only an exercise in understanding foster mothers but also one in understanding my own mother and my own mothering. I have learned about my own mothering from the foster mothers. They have demonstrated unconditional love. I have a very deep admiration for these women who work, without wages, in obscurity, in a framework of state regulations and intrusions, with children who, as one foster mother suggested, are not the "Walton Children." Yet they have a steadfast belief that what they impart to the children is worthwhile and will eventually help the foster children become physically and emotionally healthy adults—a wish all mothers have for their children.

Writing a book seems to be a solitary project, but it is not. This book would not have been possible without the assistance, advice, encouragement and support of many people. I thank them below and apologize to those whom I have forgotten to mention explicitly.

First and foremost, I thank all foster mothers in New Brunswick for their support. I feel very indebted to the foster mothers I interviewed; they gave so freely of their time considering their own busy schedules.

A sincere thanks goes to John Whipple of the New Brunswick Foster Parents Association, to Reuben Orenstein, Program Consultant, Children's Residential Resources for the New Brunswick Department of Health and Community Services, to Lois Mitchell and her family for their contributions and suggestions towards my research project on foster families, and to Barbara Pepperdene for suggestions on the manuscript.

A very sincere thanks to my friend Nancy Nason-Clark for all her advice and support. Not only was her academic knowledge important to me, but her unwavering belief in me as a person, a researcher and a friend was a great strength during this project. Also a sincere thanks to my friends Barbara Fisher-Townsend and Ann Soucy for their willingness to listen to the endless and no doubt boring stories about the project.

I also thank Errol Sharpe of Fernwood Publishing for his belief that foster mothers provide an important service and that their invisible work should be made a bit more visible.

The following institutions are acknowledged for their financial support for my Ph.D. program: the Social Sciences and Humanities Research Council of Canada, the O'Brien Foundation of St. John and the Canadian Federation of University Women for their scholarships, and the Nels Anderson Fund of the Sociology Department of the University of New Brunswick which allowed me to travel across New Brunswick to conduct the interviews.

Last, but absolutely not least, I thank my family. Ajit Thakkar, my husband, has supported me throughout my career and without his help this book would not have been possible. I thank my parents, who still live in Holland, for providing me with a warm and loving family that has allowed me to pursue any career I wanted. I am pleased to acknowledge my sister who is just a great pal and who I always have lots of fun with. I am very proud of my sons Aroon and Niels who had to compete for time with this book project.

Introduction

Molly Delaronde, born to a methadone-addicted mother, was taken to hospital with critical head injuries. Her foster mother has been charged with assault (Matas 1997:A1)

S tories like the above are common in the media. Many problems with foster care in Canada have been reported lately. The Mount Cashel hearings in 1989 in Newfoundland exposed severe abuse in foster homes (O'Brien 1991). Such media articles create the impression that foster parents are poor caregivers and that they regularly abuse the children entrusted to them. As a result, our image of foster parents is by and large a negative one. Few positive stories appear in the media, and when they do, they portray foster parents in an heroic fashion. Little is known about what really takes place in foster families. What type of work is involved in caring for a foster child? How are relationships among all the players in foster-care services, such as the caregiver, the foster child, the provincial child welfare department (the state), the biological parent(s) and foster family members constructed? The basic question this book addresses is: What happens inside the foster family?

In much of the literature on foster care the emphasis is on foster parents as the caregivers of the foster child. Foster parents are treated as a homogenous family unit in which both the male and the female are equally involved in parenting responsibilities. However, I believe this to be an erroneous approach. Research indicates that "the actual work of caring for children [in foster care] has been allocated to women" (Swift 1995:102). Furthermore, women and men's experiences are often very different from each other. As Eichler and Lapointe have argued, "since the social situation of the sexes is different, it is likely that their viewpoints on the same institutions would also be different" (1985:21). This book does support both Swift and Eichler and Lapointe by demonstrating that foster mothers are the most significant caregivers in foster families and that a family cannot be treated as one homogenous unit.

Fostering is a unique type of caregiving. It is different from nursing care or from daycare. The main difference is not the type of care but the time of care. Foster care is not a nine-to-five job. Fostering takes place on a twenty-four-hour basis in the physical space of the caregiver, very much as mother care does. Fostering is deeply rooted in mothering. Further, this book analyzes the complex web of relationships among the foster mother, child welfare services and the biological family of the foster child. It provides a glimpse, simultaneously, into foster care and mother care, through the lives of mainly working-class women.

Foster mothers occupy a unique central role in the delivery of foster-care services in Canada. Their role is shaped by their belief in mothering and carried out within a framework of provincial rules and regulations (*Child Welfare in Canada* 1994). Foster mothers are often sandwiched between the demands of the foster child, the demands of their own family members and the demands of the state. These demands not only bring conflict, they are also characterized by paradoxes and contradictions. For example, in order for a foster mother to spend time with her troubled teenaged foster child, she may have to devote less time to her own children.

The research for this book is based on twenty interviews conducted in 1994 with foster mothers in New Brunswick. Although the data was collected in New Brunswick, the issues discussed and analyzed are relevant to all foster mothers in Canada. Legislation, rules and regulations frame foster-care services differently from province to province, but what takes place *inside* the foster family and the changing intra-familial dynamics when a family becomes a foster family are relevant to *all* Canadian foster families and perhaps all foster families in North America.

Doing the interviews was a wonderful experience. Although I am a mother, I have never fostered a child. I do not share that experience with foster mothers. I agonized over whether it was ethically responsible to write a book on others. Therefore, I think it is important to explain why I decided to go ahead. Ann Oakley (1981) argues that interviewing is "morally indefensible" and the best way to interview is when the "interviewer is prepared to invest his or her personal identity in the relationship." I found it difficult to apply Oakley's model. Yes, I did talk about my personal life during the interviews; however, I was there in the first place to listen and to understand foster mothers' lived experiences. According to Amy Rossiter, the "intention of the interviewer" (1988:25) is essential. Rossiter argues that:

> [t]o my mind there are two crucial notions within the concept of intention: the notion of discovering women's experience and the notion of women speaking for themselves.... if we are to discover women's experience through hearing women speak themselves—then the work of the interviewer clearly resides in the activity of listening rather than in "putting oneself in fully." (15)

I agree with Rossiter, and my interviews were an exercise in listening and understanding the foster mothers' stories. The foster mothers themselves were very eager to tell their stories because nobody ever asked about their lives.

An interview is, of course, much more than talking to someone for a certain period of time. It is a process that starts before the actual face-to-face interview takes place. The first step was to call each participant to ask whether she was still willing to take part in the interview. Approximately three to four months had elapsed between the time the foster mothers had received the survey and returned it indicating that they would like to be interviewed, and my follow-up phone call. Many had forgotten about the project. However, after being reminded, no foster mother declined; in fact they were very eager to participate in this phase of the research.

The interviews were often held in the kitchen, and the following story describes the typical interview environment. I arrived at Annie's[1] home and was welcomed by the bark of a little dog and invited to sit at the kitchen table. I was immediately offered coffee and we talked about general things. Both of us were a bit nervous. Even though all foster mothers were very eager to participate, the relationship between any researcher and participant is always somewhat unnatural. Amy Rossiter argues:

> The unusual form of research/subject relationships has been characterized as a relationship of inequality, where the researcher's power comes from the ability to determine content, possession of extra "knowledge," and control of the methods. (1988:23)

After approximately ten minutes of general conversation which centered on the foster mothers' and my children, we started the interview. With Annie, as with almost all other foster mothers, the fact that I was a mom was a determining factor in "breaking the ice."

By far the hardest part of "doing" research is not the interviews or the writing-up of the results, but the interpretation of the data. I wanted to reflect as much as possible upon the foster mothers' stories because the intent of the research was to allow as much as possible those women to speak for themselves, but ultimately the analysis was carried out by me. As Adrienne Rich states: "You cannot speak for me. I cannot speak for us" (1986:224). I have interpreted the lives of the foster mothers in order to understand their world, their mothering, their relationships to power structures and how they make sense of their day-to-day lives. Nevertheless, the interpretation of their stories is rooted in my own complex background of lived experiences and academic knowledge. I believe that it is very important, as a researcher, to give "voice" to the research participants. I also believe that it is important to recognize the limitations of this approach (Baker 1996). In this book I will try to stay as close to the voices of the foster mothers as possible, but ultimately it is a book that describes and analyzes the lives of foster mothers through my personal lens.

NOTE

1. Annie is a fictitious name.

Chapter 1

Mothering through the Ages

In order to historically contextualize (foster) mothering, it is important to examine the concept of mothering through time. During the Middle Ages children were viewed as small adults. Infant mortality rates were high; at least 25 percent of children died before the age of five. Large numbers of illegitimate children in Europe were abandoned (Boswell 1988). Society at large, as well as parents and in particular mothers, seemed indifferent towards the plight of children, and high infant mortality rates were considered inevitable. This indifference, some social historians argue, in itself created infant mortality (Stone 1977). During the Renaissance a new attitude towards child rearing, the place of children in society and familial relationships developed. A number of conditions were responsible for people beginning to see children differently: the influence of Christianity, the forces of industrialization and the development of medical knowledge. These developments all provided the groundwork for why contemporary childcare is centred around the role of the biological mother. She is considered the most important caregiver.

THE CHANGE IN THE MOTHER ROLE

Family relationships in the Middle Ages were kin oriented but over time these relationships were influenced by the teachings of the Christian Church. Kin oriented relationships changed to reflect the hierarchy of the Church. Reflecting God the Father, the father in the family became the autocratic head of the household. Women, initially only upper-class women, were pushed towards the private sphere (Zelizer 1981; Currie 1986).

The second antecedent that influenced people's attitude towards child rearing practices and consequently the role of women was a general concern about the wellbeing of children. Slowly, women started to resist the notion that high infant mortality was inevitable. As a result, women became more involved in and attached to their own children, reducing infant mortality rates. Phillipe Aries was the first social historian to suggest that parental and societal attitudes changed towards children. He argues: "care expended on children inspired new feelings, a new emotional attitude, to which iconography of the seventeenth century gave brilliant and insistent expression: the modern concept of the family" (1962:413). Between 1660 and 1800 an extraordinary change in child rearing theory and practices, and in the affectionate relations between parents and children, took place (Stone 1977). Stone argues that this new attitude towards children and childhood occurred first in the well-to-do classes and then trickled down to the lower classes. Stone attributes the change to individual family causes. He states:

> From family to family a variety of motives may have been at work to stimulate this concern for children. In some cases, easy-going affection from a happy marriage spilled over on the children.... In others, bored young mothers found children from two to seven amazing pets.... In others, unhappily married mothers, or mothers whose beloved husbands were for years on end away ... turned all their psychic energies upon their children. (450)

Shorter (1975) supports Stone's contention that the change in child rearing attitudes and practices was caused by a change of ideas in the early part of the Renaissance. According to Shorter, well-to-do women became more and more concerned about high infant mortality and as a result ceased the practice of sending their children to wet-nurses. By the middle of the seventeenth century most upper-class women breast-fed their own children, which ensured a higher survival rate. This of course had an impact on lower-class women, and in any case fewer lower-class women were able to buy the services of a wet-nurse. The result of all this, Shorter argues, is that women started to develop powerful emotional ties with their infants.

Furthermore, not only women and parents but the society at large expressed concern about child rearing practices. Aries states that church leaders and other pedagogues grew increasingly concerned about the morals and vices children were exposed to.

> Towards the end of the sixteenth century a more obvious change took place; certain pedagogues, whose ideas were to carry weight and who would succeed in imposing their concepts and scruples on others, refused to allow children to be given indecent books any longer. This was a very important stage, which may be regarded as marking the beginning of respect for childhood (1962:109).

Badinter (1981) argues that the change in attitude towards children was strongly influenced by the fact that large groups of literate middle-class women followed Jean Jacques Rousseau's teachings on health and nutrition for pregnant and nursing women. Rousseau advocated that mothers should be actively involved in ensuring that their infants grew up in a healthy environment. The important message that Rousseau taught these women was that they could influence their environment, and that not all illnesses and poor health were entirely the result of God, the Devil or the Evil Eye.

In addition, colonialization also provided an impetus to "preserve" children. French officials were convinced that "France was becoming depopulated" (Badinter 1981:122). This was a concern because people were needed to extract the "great reservoirs of wealth" in the colonies (126; also Donzelot 1979). Suddenly high infant mortality rates were seen as a problem. Attempts were made to "try to remedy the causes of the waste of human potential" (Badinter 1981:123).

French state officials devised a plan for abandoned children to populate and work in the new colonies. The plan was

> [to export] children (well fed before on cow's milk) to Louisiana at the age of five or six years. The different crops they could farm, depending on their age and

strength, would provide "an enormous profit and cover essential needs." (Badinter 1981:127)

Thus in France, abandoned children became an asset to the state instead of a liability. To maximize profit for the state, these children should survive rather than die. The economic potential of (poor) children became the driving force to improve their lot.

Thus a number of different factors, such as the increased number of women who nursed their own children, the subsequent bonding, the overall notion that children were not really little adults and should not be exposed to all types of adult behaviour, the desire to populate the colonies, and the teachings of Rousseau steered women towards the role of the sole, private caregiver of their own children. However, the strongest societal forces that shaped the role of women were the development of medical knowledge and industrialization.

THE IMPACT OF THE NEW MEDICAL PROFESSION

The development of the medical profession was perhaps the most powerful force that committed women to the private sphere. Initially, the impact of the fledgling profession was most noticeable on middle- and upper-class women and their children, but later middle-class norms were often forced upon working-class women. The doctors focused their services on the middle- and upper-middle classes simply because they were able to pay for the service. It was in the late seventeenth century, according to Stone, that English physical sciences started to challenge "traditional ideas" about the universe (1977:232). A major breakthrough was the development of a smallpox vaccine.

> In 1774 Dr. Lettson drew attention to medical improvements which contributed to the same effect, in particular inoculation against smallpox, better obstetrics training of midwives, and improvements in the nurture and management of infants. (477).

People felt that they did not have to accept their fate passively any more. Another important area the medical profession concentrated on was childbirth[1]. Many women died in childbirth and the "plague of the puerperal fever" claimed more women's lives than ever before (Rich 1986). According to Rich "[t]he real issue, underlying the economic profit of the medical profession, is the mother's relation to childbirth, an experience in which women have historically felt out of control and at the mercy of biology, fate, or change" (145).

The new professionals soon made themselves indispensable, inadvertently creating more problems for women. Additionally, doctors expressed concern about the wellbeing of children after they were born (Aries 1962; Shorter 1975; Badinter 1981). In order to treat upper- and middle-class children successfully, doctors realized that they needed an ally. They focused their attention on mothers; the doctors felt that mothers, rather than servants or wet-nurses, were the best persons to keep children healthy and raise them in an environment sanctioned by the medical profession.

Childbearing was "no longer just a matter of producing an optimum number of children, but one of correct management" (Gordon 1980:172). The medical professions wanted to educate parents about the care of children. Thus "the family [became] the target for a great enterprise of medical acculturation" (173).

The alliance between mothers and doctors benefited both groups. It extended the power base of the doctors; they were legitimized by the most powerful class in society, allowing doctors to consolidate knowledge and power as a professional group. Middle-class women were educated in how better to care for their children, which increased their power in the family (Donzelot 1979; Badinter 1981). This was of particular importance because women were now seen as the primary persons responsible for their children. Donzelot argues:

> with the mothers' help, the doctor prevailed against the stubborn hegemony of that popular medicine of old wives, and on the other hand, owing to the increased importance of maternal functions, he conceded a new power to the bourgeois woman in the domestic sphere. (1979:20)

Thus the developing medical profession and upper- and middle-class women created a somewhat symbiotic relationship: the women felt they needed the doctors in order to survive childbirth and to raise their infants, while the doctors needed the women to legitimize their profession. This powerful alliance propelled women into the role of the sole caregiver of their children. This mutually beneficial relationship between women and doctors was not for poor women as they could not afford to consult a physician. For these women child rearing practices and their own changing roles were more the consequence of legislation that resulted from the impact of industrialization.

THE IMPACT OF INDUSTRIALIZATION

Industrialization had a major effect on working-class people's lives and values (Goode 1963). Children of the poor and working classes had always been economic assets to their families. When their age allowed, they worked with the family to produce the necessities of life. Tilly et al. argued that "[m]en, women, and children worked at tasks which were differentiated by age and sex, but the work of all was necessary for survival," because the "family was the unit of productive activity" (1978:293). When the children's labour was not needed at home they were sent off as servants, but they still contributed to the family .

Industrialization changed the working conditions of children dramatically (Synott 1984:133). In the new wage economy all members of the family, including children, had to work outside the home in order to make a (minimum) living wage (Ursel 1992; Nett 1988; Mackie 1984). Although children were cheap labour, they remained an important source of income for the family (Stone 1977). Tilly et al. state:

> Agricultural change drove rural labourers and peasants city-ward at the end of the eighteenth century, and technological change drove many artisans and their families [including children] into the ranks of the unskilled. (1978:295)

Many children worked under terrible conditions (Nett 1988; Stone 1977; Hiley 1979). Some children as young as four years old worked in factories. The working conditions of girls in the mines in the nineteenth century were described as horrendous. Half-naked girls were dragging corfs loaded with coal through narrow passageways. The first report of the Children's Employment Commission On Mines in 1842 described in detail the conditions under which girls had to work (Hiley 1979). "The chain, passing high up between the legs of two of these girls, had worn large holes in their trousers, and any sight more disgustingly indecent or revolting can scarcely be imagined than these girls at work" (51).

Many working-class and poor children died as a result of industrialization (Synott 1984). Some died of poor working conditions and others died at home due to accidents because working parents had to leave them alone. In addition, unsanitary, cramped, urban living quarters were a breeding ground for contagious and infectious diseases for all. The mortality rates among children from the working class were often higher than pre-industrialization rates (Mackie 1984:40). As a result of these terrible working and living conditions, Badinter (1981) argued that poor women just could not afford to be too loving towards their children. Stone argued that "parental love ... was hardly conducive to early industrial work" (1977:663).

Industrialization, initially, had a very negative impact on poor and working-class families. Child rearing practices, which had changed for middle- and upper-class children, did not change for the poor and working classes. In fact working-class children were far worse off than in the pre-industrial era. In the meantime, middle- and upper-class children enjoyed the "Victorian golden age" (Synott 1984). When report after report was published about the appalling working conditions for children, action was initiated by the bourgeois classes. In England, the first *Factory Act* was passed in 1833 (Synott 1984; Mackie 1984). This new Act stated that children under the age of six were not permitted to work, and children between the ages of six and ten were not allowed to work more than sixteen hours a day.

In France, the state was also concerned about child workers. The fear was that poor working people and "vagabonds" could become a political force. This had to be curtailed by educating them in the "rhythms" of the working world. Thus according to Meyer the goals of education were meant to mold "a population which lived by the rhythm of the street" into workers, accustomed to working in factories so as to avoid riots and political turmoil (Meyer 1977:7).

In Canada, just like in Europe, the state became more and more involved with the plight of the workers. Unbridled capitalism had created dreadful working conditions. In 1871, women and children comprised 42 percent of the Canadian labour force. Through the influx of immigrants there was a large surplus of labour, driving all wages down (Ursel 1992). The low wages and deplorable conditions, in particular for women and children, sparked the founding of social-reform movements by the middle class. Although these movements were concerned about the poor working conditions of women and children, they also were interested in stabilizing reproductive relations (Ursel 1992). In the late nineteenth- and early part of the twentieth-century, working women were perceived by middle-class women's organizations as a "social crisis, creating problems of cleanliness, morality and health for future mothers" (White 1993:3). That these women had to work to survive was ignored. Unions in general also ignored the role of women in the workplace. According to White, women were actively excluded from unions. Unions advocated the abolition of child labour for children under fourteen and the removal of women from the labour force. The unions argued that "the great principle for which we fight is opposed to taking ... women from their homes to put them in the factory and in sweatshops" (1993:23). The abolition of child labour and the exclusion of women from unions was not entirely based on noble ideas but was more rooted in unions members' fear that they could not compete with the low wages paid to women and children. Instead of advocating for decent wages for all workers, unions advocated for a family wage so that women and children did not need to work. The result was that women workers' interests were completely disregarded and many worked for half of the wages of their male counterparts. For example, in 1907, male bookbinders in Vancouver earned $13.50 and female bookbinders earned $5.25 a week (White 1993:35). The exclusion of women from unions and their poor working conditions drove them even more readily into the private unpaid sphere of childcare and domestic work.

Legislative acts curtailed the hours children could work in shops and mines. Mandatory schooling facilitated the process of prolonged childhood. Just as with child labour laws, mandatory schooling was not enacted to support children but was instituted to assist the industries. The capitalist, in order to have a competent workforce, needed workers who could read and write (Gomme 1995). Zelizer argues that "children were removed from the market between 1870 and 1930 in large part because it had become more economical and efficient to educate them than to hire them" (1981:112). With a prolonged childhood, children became a financial liability, and working-class mothers, who were excluded from unions and therefore from decent wages, became housewives with the responsibility to raise the children and to maintain the male worker. This meant working long hours for no wages while being financially dependent on their husbands. Just as for middle- and upper-class women, working-class women became the designated child rearers.

THE MYTH OF MOTHERHOOD

The "stay at home mother" is a social construct developed over the last two centuries. The result is that biological mothers are deemed to be the best caregivers for their children. Moreover, mothering became idealized. Mothers are often portrayed as single dimensional people who are "loving, gentle, tender, self-sacrificing, devoted, [with a] limited interest ... creating a haven for her family" (Bernard in Kaplan 1992:6). The problem with this image is that it collides with the reality of women's lives. For example, many women do not enjoy mothering as their sole vocation (Rich 1986; Meyer 1985). Nevertheless, the social support for the "myth of motherhood" is strong and was augmented by some social theorists.

Many early functionalists supported and propagated the "myth of motherhood." According to Parsons (1959), it is not in the best interests of society that women join the workforce. It is important that only the breadwinner—the male—works for wages. Women competing for jobs would cause tension in the family. In any case, according to the functionalist paradigm, one needs different characteristics for the public and private spheres. In the workforce one has to be competitive and aggressive while in the family one has to be caring and nurturing. These conflicting roles require a segregation by gender. Parsons states:

the dominant mature feminine role is that of housewife or of wife and mother. Apart from the extremely important utilitarian problems of how adequate care of households and children are to be accomplished, the most important aspect of this fact is that it shields spouses from competing with each other in the occupational sphere, which, along with attractiveness to women, is above all the most important single focus of feelings of self-respect on the part of American men. (1959:265)

This view of mothers has not served women well. Meyer argues that "defining and even regarding women with sentiment as primarily nurturing or mothering has important personal, social, economic and political consequences" (1985:250). Women and mothers have been left out of the power structures and have been restricted to the private realm. Meg Luxton argues that on an individual level there may be the will to change these patterns, but on a structural level there is little support for change. "Very few unions have won paternity leave ... so it is very difficult for new fathers to get time off work to be with their new children" (1995:299).

Not only are women and their mothering roles marginalized, children also suffer from marginalization. "Whether recipients of AFDC [welfare in the United States] on the school lunch line, at the soup kitchen, using food stamps, living in unspeakable housing ... children are only as well off as their mothers" (Meyer 1985:250). Regardless of the living circumstances in which women are forced to raise their children, they are always held responsible for the failure to raise "good" children. Women are seen as causing "schizophrenia, homosexuality, juvenile delinquency, and a host of other social 'problems'" (Forcey 1987:27).

Not only has the image of the "good" mother (the caring, compassionate, self-sacrificing, middle-class woman with good housekeeping skills) been constructed (Swift 1995; Margolis 1984), so has the image of the "bad" mother. The failed mother is an important social construct in the context of foster care, because it is the "good" (foster) mother who typically rescues the child from the "bad" (biological) mother. Swift (1995) has demonstrated that the notion of a bad mother is often based on considerations which have more to do with conformity than with issues of neglect and abuse, i.e., non-conforming mothers are more easily accused of neglecting their children than conforming mothers. Moreover, in many cases of neglect, even if the father plays an active role in that neglect, it is the mother who is mostly held responsible[2].

In addition, the label "bad" mother is more easily attached to poorer mothers. External socio-economic factors are rarely taken into consideration in the judgement. Child neglect is seen as an individual problem of a failed mother instead of, as is often the case, a problem of poverty and other social circumstances (Swift 1995). In fact, poor women have a much greater chance of being investigated for child neglect if they do not fit the middle-class/ popular media notion of a woman/mother. They are frequently judged on their appearance and mannerisms. For example, when Swift examined child neglect case files, she found the following description of a mother who allegedly had neglected her children: "Mom is slow, overweight, had dirty hair. She was wearing a tight T-shirt, obviously braless which was totally inappropriate for the large bosomed frame (108)." This woman's physical appearance implicated her in the neglect of her children. Swift argues that "on the surface we see a picture of 'poor care,' that is, care deemed unacceptable by personnel mandated to act by sets of sanctioned social processes" (172). However, in the same case files, Swift found that the physical appearance of the fathers was hardly ever described or judged.

Child neglect is often the subjective experience of the social worker who, with a different value system than the women being investigated, sees neglect when in actuality it is poverty or some other factor they see. Thus mothers are not only judged on the type and quality of care they provide, they are measured against an ideal of what a woman/mother should be. In many cases, failed mothers are constructed from information other than their actual caring practices and are measured against middle-class values.

Feminist literature on mothering is somewhat bifurcated, relying on either a social construction or a biological explanation of it. Neo-conservative and liberal feminism both argue that women's mothering is inevitable and that society should strive to make it as rewarding as possible without changing the patriarchical structures (Descarries-Belanger and Roy 1991). On the other hand, feminists grounded in psychoanalysis and radical thought argue that mothering is socially constructed. Nancy Chodorow (1978) states that mothering is a culturally learned activity, not solely the result of biology. Chodorow sees mothering as the outcome of a psychological process, whereby the role is conveyed differently to sons and daughters. Radical feminists see motherhood as being exclusively socially constructed and the inevitable ultimate outcome of patriarchy (Tong 1989). The goal for women, according to radical feminists, should be to abolish motherhood as an institution and as their domestic responsibility (Descarries-Belanger and Roy 1991). They focus their inquiry on the various social aspects of exploitation, originating in the relations between biological and social reproduction, and on the subjective division of public and private domains.

Barrett and McIntosh (1991) argue that we live in a familialized society, with the nuclear family and the stay-at-home mother who takes sole responsibility for raising the children as the most dominant and important institution in society. As a result, popular culture frequently produces an unrealistic and idealized version of the family, a myth that is extremely popular. "Familialism is not a ruling-class or patriarchical ideology repressively foisted on the unwilling population" (210). The popularity of the family rests on a number of notions: "the emotional security that the family brings to its members (relationships are based on ascription and not choice); the notion that the two-parent-family is the best place to raise children; and the more abstract notion that the family is naturally given and is socially and morally desirable" (27). While recognizing the "popularity" of the traditional family, they are very critical of the current Western "familialized society" because it does not serve women and children well, but instead serves patriarchy and capitalism. The human needs for "affection, security, intimacy, sexual love, parenthood," which are strongly associated with and used to justify the family, are genuine needs, but they can also be met in other constructs "in a more genuine context" than the traditional family (133). Barrett and McIntosh suggest two general objectives for change in the family: first, political changes to allow more alternatives to the existing family patterns, and second, a move away from individualism toward collectivism for certain recurring household tasks.

Foster care based on the functionalist notion that women are the best caregivers of children or the model of the "good" mother is one of the cornerstones of family child welfare services in Canada. But how do foster mothers, women who mother other women's children by choice, explain their own lives and activities? How do these women see their own mothering?

NOTES

1. Childbirth had always been a risky business for women; many women died in childbirth. In the seventeenth century, men got more involved in obstetric practices, and they unknowingly created a crisis that made their profession more needed. The involvement of men, going from one childbirth to another with invasive techniques such as the forceps and manual manipulation, created the "plague of the puerperal fever." This fever killed many women. In one year in the province of Lombardy, France, not a single woman survived childbirth (Rich 1986:116–17).

2. For example, in the well-publicized case of the middle-class couple in the United States that left their four- and seven-year-old daughters at home when they went on vacation to Mexico, it was the mother who had failed (Swift 1995). In the case of the very seriously abused and neglected child in New Brunswick (who died as a result), it was the mother who was held more responsible for the neglect of the child in the popular media, although both parents received the same prison sentence (*The Daily Gleaner*, May 31, 1995).

Chapter 2

Is Foster Care Mother Care?

THE DEVELOPMENT OF FOSTER CARE IN CANADA

Because of the needs of the medical profession and the demands of industrialization, women and their children were relegated to the private sphere. Families who did not adhere to this new model of family needed to be "educated." Poor families often could not afford for the mother to stay at home and care for the children. The phenomenon of poor children roving the streets was interpreted as the result of "the failure of the family environment" instead of the failure of society to provide adequate living conditions (Meyer 1977:23). This allowed the state to label some families as irregular or dysfunctional. The fledgling medical profession was quick to add its voice to support such labelling. According to the new medical sciences, "the offspring [should be] the gravitational centre" of the family (40). If a family failed to treat the children as the "gravitational centre" they were deemed to produce maladjusted children in need of protection. The new middle-class child-rearing practices and the emerging medical "knowledge" created the conditions for the basis of state family intervention as we know it today.

The defined need for intervention created the profession of social worker, who, on behalf of charity organizations and later on behalf of the state, intervened in dysfunctional families. The social work profession became a powerful force attached to many institutions, such as "the judiciary, public assistance, [and] the education system" (Donzelot 1979:96). The treatment of the child became the focus of these interventions, even though adults were often the target (Meyer 1977). The intense scrutiny, by the state, of families with "maladjusted" children became a tool for imposing the middle class and state's model on all families (Meyer 1977; Donzelot 1979).

The development of child welfare services in Canada exemplifies Meyer and Donzelot's contention that the professionalization of medical and social practitioners fuelled state intervention in the family. For example, in Saint John, New Brunswick, a committee representing the Moral and Social Reform Council of New Brunswick, founded the Children's Aid Society in December 1912 (Young 1964). Frequently the families in "need" of intervention were very poor and their lifestyle was closely scrutinized. One family was described as having an "intemperate father and a mentally weak mother." The "mother ... was out until a late hour, and the father was home drunk" (Young 1964:5).

The number of professional social workers that assisted children apprehended from "irregular" families has increased steadily over the years, even though child welfare services developed on a "piecemeal basis" in Canada. English Canada's child welfare services were modelled after the poor laws of England, while for Quebec and part of New Brunswick the Catholic tradition of the church being responsible for poor and abandoned children was adopted (Hepworth 1980). It was recognized, in the late nineteenth century, that a more systematic approach was needed to protect children; as a result, Children's Aid Societies (CAS) were founded. Over time, as governments grew more powerful, they became more and more involved in caring for poor, abandoned and destitute children. Gradually, in the first part of the twentieth century, private Children's Aid Societies were subsumed under provincial government services or amalgamated into provincial departments. For example, in New Brunswick, Alberta, Newfoundland and Nova Scotia, provincial governments assumed complete responsibility for child welfare services. In Ontario the *Child and Family Services Act* mandates that the Minister of Community and Social Services is responsible for child welfare. This mandate is carried out by the fifty-four Children's Aid Societies in addition to a "wide range of private profit and non-profit groups and organizations" (Canada 1994:83). In British Columbia child welfare services are the responsibility of the provincial government; however, this mandate is also carried out with the assistance of private agencies.

Not only are the child welfare services carried out differently in the various provinces, the age at which a person is considered a "child" is not the same across the ten Canadian provinces. In Newfoundland and Ontario, under the child protection legislation, a child is a person under sixteen years of age; in New Brunswick[1] and British Columbia, under nineteen years; and in all the other provinces, under eighteen.

CURRENT FOSTER-CARE SERVICES IN CANADA

Foster-care services in Canada[2] have undergone dramatic changes in the last twenty years: children who enter care are older and exhibit more serious problems than before, and fewer families are willing to foster (New Brunswick 1990b:17; Ontario 1990). Since the late 1950s foster care has been the "single most important childcare resource" (Hepworth 1980:95). Across Canada, most of the children in the care of child welfare agencies are cared for in foster homes. The Prairie provinces had the highest percentage of children in the care of the state in foster care: Saskatchewan had 80 percent, Manitoba 67 percent and Alberta 58 percent. British Columbia had the lowest percentage, 44 percent, of children in foster care. In March 1992, a total of 46,251 children across Canada were in the care of child welfare services (Canada 1994). More current numbers are not easily available because foster care is provincially administered and foster-care data are not nationally compiled. "We keep better track of used cars than we do of children," says Judy Grove, executive director of the Adoption Council of Canada" (Jones 1998:53).

Although foster care is the backbone of child welfare services in Canada, in the last thirty years, every province has had difficulties in recruiting foster mothers. In 1986 New Brunswick had more than nine hundred families providing foster care, but in 1994 this number dwindled to less than seven hundred families (New Brunswick 1990b:17). In 1988 foster parents in several Ontario Children's Aid Societies threatened to go on strike to protest their "working conditions." They complained that they were a cheap "dumping ground for society's problem children" (Kendrick 1990:4). They demanded more financial compensation and more support for their services.

Foster care in Canada is in crisis, and two of the major reasons for this are: 1) changes in policy and 2) shifting opportunities for women to provide care services in their homes. First, in the last ten to fifteen years many child welfare services have adopted the policy of trying to keep the biological family together as long as possible. As a consequence, when children do enter care, they have been exposed longer to a severely dysfunctional environment, and they are often more traumatized than the foster children who entered care before this policy was put in place. Therefore, the demands on foster mothers are much higher than they were in the past, and they need "a more extensive repertoire of skills than in the past" (Ontario 1990:20). Second, when women want to provide some sort of care in their homes, they have more attractive options at their disposal, for example, home care programs for the elderly or child home-daycare. The elderly may be emotionally easier to care for and children in home-daycare programs are picked up by 6.00 pm. "[I]n light of increasing competition for the services of potential foster parents from other services that can be carried out in the home but do not carry the same twenty-four-hour-a-day stresses, such as supervised private-home daycare, foster care has to be made more attractive for it to survive" (Ontario 1990:24). In short, women who want to provide care inside their home have more attractive options available.

To forestall foster parents from closing their doors prematurely and to deter too much dependence on more costly and sometimes less effective care, such as group homes, an overhaul of foster-care services is an ongoing process in many provinces. One solution proposed to abate the crisis in foster care is to professionalize the services. Such professionalization of foster services would translate into major changes in three areas: training, remuneration and responsibilities (New Brunswick 1992). At the moment the fees paid to foster mothers differ considerably from province to province; however, the fees do not constitute a wage by any means. In New Brunswick foster mothers receive "room and board" fees: $7 per day for children five and younger, $8.50 for children between six and eleven years of age and $10 for children between eleven and nineteen. In addition foster families receive three seasonal clothing allowances of approximately $160 per child. In Ontario foster mothers receive a fee of $24 per day.

In Alberta the per diem rate ranges from $13 for an infant to $22 for a teenager between sixteen and seventeen. In addition, foster mothers can increase their per diem rate by $4.50 to $23, depending on the level of their training and how they are assessed. In British Columbia the average per diem fee is $22 for children under twelve, and $25 for children between twelve and nineteen. The hourly "wage" for these women is less than a dollar. In fact the fee may just cover the real cost of caring for a foster child, and in some cases not even that.

Nevertheless many foster mothers and some professional social workers are reluctant "to press the notion of better compensation [for their services] for fear that their motives for fostering will be misconstrued" (Ontario 1990:24; Lemay 1991). Others are unequivocal advocates of "'professional' foster parents ... [who] would function in this role just as any professional would" (Meyer 1985:257).

On a theoretical level there are also demands for the reconceptualization of foster-care services. There is a strong move to make biological parents an integral part of foster care, with the foster mother/family at the centre. Some studies indicate that foster parents' involvement with the biological parents is a very positive step. The Shared Care Program in Australia has as its aim to "confront the negative stereotype of the biological parent and the exploitation of the foster mother, and to explore the benefits of women working together" (Smith 1991). The nature of the program is that the foster mother welcomes and supports the biological mother as much as possible so as to avoid pitting themselves "against each other as 'good' or 'bad' mothers" (176). Instead the biological mother is perceived to be in need of a break from parenting responsibilities and also in need of training in parenting skills. The program is considered successful because the agency's restoration rate (child returned permanently to the biological family) was 90 percent compared to the regular rate of 57 percent.[3]

Building on the same notion of foster mothers' involvement with the natural parents is the idea proposed by Kathleen Kufeldt (1991 and 1994). Her reconceptualization of foster-care services is called "inclusive care." Inclusive care places emphasis on educating and/or helping the natural parents to cope with their children. Kufeldt argues that in order for inclusive care to be competent and productive "there needs to be a shift to a different paradigm: rather than conceptualizing the interventions as placement of the child in a substitute family, we need to reconceptualize in terms of a new and enlarged role-set consisting of the child, both families, [biological and foster] and a social worker" (Kufeldt 1994:85). In other words, Kufeldt calls for a "paradigm shift" to include the natural parents in the foster caregivers' daily activities and to see foster families as other than substitute caregivers to avoid creating "good" versus dysfunctional families. Nonetheless, inclusive foster care is premised on the theoretical notion that the biological parents are the best caregivers for their own offspring.[4]

BECOMING A FOSTER MOTHER

Although the process of becoming a foster mother/family will be different from province to province in some of the details, in general the overall process is the same across Canada.[5] A foster parent is considered "an adult who, as part of his family, cares for a child on behalf of the Minister" and a foster family provides "the child with the stability of a substitute family" (New Brunswick nd). To become a foster family, all adult members of the family have to go through a rigorous screening process including a criminal record check (New Brunswick 1990a:4). Prospective foster mothers have to attend training sessions and all adult members of the potential foster family are interviewed at least twice and the children once (New Brunswick 1990a:5).

A home study assessment examines the motivation of the foster family to foster, the physical home requirements, the personal characteristics of the potential foster family members and the expected impact of fostering on the family's own children (6). Some of the characteristics the assessor is looking for in a foster family are that a foster family be a "close-knit healthy family" wherein the members are "non-possessive" towards the foster child, have "warmth" and are "empathic," show "understanding" and have "patience, self-confidence, humility, consistency, and a sense of humor" (Orenstein 1989:238). It is also expected that "all family members … must accept and participate, to the extent of their abilities, in the program" (238). When the application has been accepted and a child has been placed with the family, a social worker carries out frequent checks or follow-up services (New Brunswick 1989). The social worker also has the obligation to oversee and evaluate the family annually for the first two years and then bi-annually (New Brunswick 1990a:Sec.4-1). If a foster family goes through major changes such as a move, change in marital status or a "substantial change" in financial matters, the foster home must be re-evaluated (s4-2). To become foster mothers, women have to go through an extensive and rigorous process, and to endure close scrutiny, not only for themselves but also for their immediate family members.

WHO ARE FOSTER MOTHERS?

Who are these women who are willing to subject themselves and their families to an intensive assessment process to evaluate whether they are suitable to care for other women's children? This study's data makes it possible to create a profile of them. All but 13 percent of foster mothers were married with the rest being single, widowed, divorced, separated or living in common-law relationships. These numbers reflect the unstated assumption that foster families should be "traditional" families i.e., hetero-sexual married couples.

The average age of foster mothers was forty-three years. Most of them still have some or all of their own children living at home. In general, foster mothers' own children were teenagers with an average age of nineteen years. Foster mothers and their families lived predominantly in rural areas (81 percent) and the vast majority (89 percent) reported involvement in religion ranging from Roman Catholicism to Pentecostal.

More than half of the foster mothers were "stay-at-home" women (55 percent). One quarter of the foster mothers worked outside the home full-time and a further 20 percent worked outside the home part-time. The occupations they practised ranged from hairdresser and short-order cook to managerial. On an educational level, almost half of the foster mothers had finished high school (48 percent), while nearly a quarter (23 percent) had some post-secondary education ranging from community college to university.

Of the spouses of the foster mothers, the majority worked

outside the home (64 percent), 17 percent worked part-time and the rest were unemployed or retired. The occupation or profession practised by the foster mothers' spouses was wide ranging, from labourer to university professor. What was very interesting was that, on average, the educational level of the spouses was lower than that of foster mothers. Almost half of the foster mothers had finished high school compared with 36 percent of the spouses.

Finally, fostering was a longterm commitment for many foster mothers. The women who responded to the survey had been fostering for seven years on average. They had cared for an average of thirteen foster children during their individual fostering careers. Thus the foster mothers of this study did not abandon fostering easily once they got involved.

Foster mothers in this study, it can be concluded, belong to traditional, mostly rural families where the parents were married with some children still living at home and a husband who worked outside the home. Foster mothers were by and large housewives who had a religious affiliation and an average high school education, who once committed to fostering, tended to stay with it.

TYPE OF CARE PROVIDED

Foster mothers in this study experienced some degree of role confusion with respect to the nature of the care they provided to children who are not their own. For some foster mothers, particularly those who cared for handicapped children, there were specific requirements and skills that enabled them to meet the health needs of the foster children. These mothers had little difficulty referring to the care they provided as "professional care." However, during the interviews women described and discussed their care almost exclusively in terms of mothering, with references such as "mother love" and "mother care," even though some women had stated that the care they provided was both professional and family-based care. Almost all twenty foster mothers interviewed located their caring almost exclusively within the domestic domain during the interview. In fact the discussion during the interview about the type of care provided created some bewilderment. For example, one conversation went as follows:

Interviewer: You mentioned in your survey that the care you provide is mostly family-based care. Can you describe a bit of what you mean by family-based care?

1307: How was the question worded? Was it worded differently?

Interviewer: The question asked in the survey was: "Do you feel that you provide family-based care, or professional-based care or both?" I was just wondering if you can describe what you mean by family-based care?

1307: I think I remember. It was kind of like are you the mother and father at home or are you basically the babysitter. I am providing the necessities, I am providing a home.... I feel I am providing a home ... where the kids belong, as where my kids belonged. I am here, I put the meals on the table, do the laundry.

This type of exchange was not uncommon. The most frequent descriptions foster mothers offered about their care referred to how foster children were integrated into the new family unit: "I treat them like my own" or "[I] make them part of the family." One foster mother explained it this way:

We just do as a family would do, as we always do. I'm a mom. I make sure that they are out of bed in the morning, I make sure that they are clean, I make sure that they have plenty to eat, I make sure that they are happy. If they're down, I do things, that's it. There is nothing more, there is just family. There is no other way to say it, that's it. I just take care of them.... That is what I mean by family, it is based on an everyday routine thing. The love and care and all the things that go with it and they are no different than my own kids. (1320)

Another foster mother described her experiences:

you make them a part of your family. Don't make them an outcast. Don't treat them as the outsider. You try and integrate them as much into your family activities, into things that they like to do. You do it as a family and it is every day you go on as a family. This is how you do it.... They need protection, they need to be loved, they need to be accepted, they need to know that they are okay. They need their self-confidence and their self-esteem back and you treat them as family. They are family and you treat them as family. (1047)

The most important characteristic foster mothers felt they needed for the job was an abundance of love and patience. As one foster mother explained: "I have a lot of love to give and I love kids. I have been babysitting since I was twelve and I love kids. It is hard on the nerves at times, but I love kids." Many foster mothers found it difficult to describe what it took to be a foster mother.

Few foster mothers felt that fostering was much more than mothering. One foster mother explained:

Well I do everything. I do all the doctoring, I do nursing, I bring the children home from hospital when they would normally not even let them out.... I never ask for relief, I never ask for a weekend off. I never get special allowances, I do it straight [for] $7 [a day] like everybody else and yet I am doing twenty-four-hour nursing, I'm doing a lot of psychological work because I am trying to mend fences and make them whole again. I make them so that they can go out onto the street and hold their own. I think I do anyway. I also prepare my own family to go out there and hold their head up high and stand up for what they believe in and not be afraid to cry. I try to stress there is nothing wrong with being human. I think I do, I do all the same things, I just don't have the letters after my name. I do so much more for my foster children than I ever did for my own because they need so much more. They don't need just a simple mother. They need you to solve so many little things that aren't little.... Even when policemen are here interviewing because of charges that have been laid.... All the while you are trying to just be a simple ordinary mother and there is nothing simple about it. You have to be aware legally of what you are doing,

there is just so many things people don't really understand. It is hard to understand, it is just hard. (1167)

Many foster mothers felt that mothering skills come naturally
when women bear children; that mothering was not a learned
activity. The more technical skills (such as tube-feeding a handicapped child) that were acquired through training programs
were more easily viewed by foster mothers as "professional"
skills. Foster mothers in general felt that they provided care to
foster children by drawing upon their experiences as a mother. In
short, they were first and foremost mothers to their foster children. They were not counsellors, they were not therapists, they
were not teachers. They were mothers and they mothered the
foster child. Although the women had some difficulty describing
exactly what they meant by mothering, it encompassed a multi-
tude of different tasks including physical care (cooking, laundry,
etc.) for the child, representing the child's interests and protect-
ing the child from others.

FOSTER MOTHERS AND BIOLOGICAL PARENTS
One of the major features of the professionalization of foster-care
services is that foster mothers will have increased interactions
with the foster child's biological parents, as suggested by Kufeldt.
On a theoretical level, this approach may be attractive; however,
foster mothers need to be convinced of the usefulness of this
paradigm shift. The analysis of the interview data casts doubt on
the workability of this policy. All foster mothers interviewed,
except for one, reported ambivalent feelings about the relationship with the foster child's natural parents. By and large, the
women would rather not have any contact with the foster child's
parents or other family members, even though they recognized
that if the reunification of the family was to have any chance of
success, the foster children had to have continued contact with
their parents and/or family. However, as a group, the foster
mothers were very skeptical about family reunification, particularly when the foster child's family was not offered any assistance
to solve their original problems. As one foster mother explained:
"I was trying to explain to social services that, how can you fix a
problem just by removing the children and putting the children

back six months later without those parents having been helped?" She went on to argue that:

> Natural parents definitely have to be in the picture more so than anything. The only thing that I do say is: "This is my safe haven [home], this is the child's safe haven. No parents will ever enter whether it be with good will or bad will!" (1079)

Few foster mothers seemed to enjoy contact with the foster children's parents. They endured the contact because they felt that they had no choice; the court and/or the social worker had ordered the visits.

There were a number of other reasons why foster mothers did not like contact with the foster child's family. Sometimes the foster mothers felt unsafe when they had to interact with a parent who was perceived to be violent. Some foster mothers felt apprehension and fear when the biological parents knew where they lived. One foster mother in particular feared for her foster daughter's safety. She explained:

> our daughter's father unfortunately knows where I live ... he is not to come within so many feet of her and not to try anything because he knows that he is going to be in the wrong and if he does then he will be handled. She doesn't know about her mom because she was very young and her mom just left her, that was it. It is okay to have contact with the natural parents, but I feel that sometimes they know a little bit too much. They are only told so much but yet they go upon themselves to seek out more.... It makes me feel a little unsafe at times knowing that maybe if she drives up and down the road on her bike what could happen. (1247)

This fear was exacerbated by the fact that foster mothers felt that many biological families saw the foster family as the "enemy," people who had taken their child away.

Furthermore, foster mothers felt strongly that their role was to protect the foster child. Many foster children were distressed when they returned from a visit with their family. For a couple of days after the visit, the foster children were often difficult to handle. Above all, the children were sad, depressed or angry because the visit did not work out the way they had anticipated.

Some foster mothers were particularly upset when they were required to have contact with the foster child's parents when the parents had abused that child. One foster mother explained her feelings and actions:

> The only time it bothers me is when I know that there was abuse. It bothers me, especially if that child is going to go back. I mean that's horror to me. I don't think enough is done before they are put back. Really, that is the only scary thing. We have one daughter that we have adopted. She was going to be placed back and I knew that when she came. It was just horrible, a horrible thought and we got involved with adoption and we did finally adopt her and she is still with us. She was mentally handicapped and there was a lot of abuse that was never even mentioned and it was horrifying, I don't even like to talk about it. (1327)

Another foster mother felt that the natural parents had lost their right to parent their own children. She stated:

> these people have lost their right to parent. They lost that right, they proved themselves unfit. I don't want any contact with them; it will only make my job worse because the child is not going to respect me and listen to my rules if they can keep going back to the natural parents. It won't work. (1047)

Another foster mother explained:

> We are here for the children not for the parents. I feel that it is not my problem but the social worker or something like that. I am here for the children. (1591)

Only one of the twenty foster mothers enjoyed having contact with the foster children's mothers. She explained:

> There are some I could not get in contact with. I do not have any problem with that. Some [biological] parents stay with us over the weekend or Christmas. That is after [we had] the children for a year. I have [L] over and I had [N] over three times. However [other foster child] turned around and said: "I will invite my father over." We said: "No no. No males in here." Her father drinks too much and we do not drink.... We have to get to know them first. One biological mother has a drinking problem, but we told her, the first time she came down, we had a barbecue and people will be drinking. But if you are coming, you cannot be drinking. (1209)

This foster mother was very much the exception. In most cases, it seemed that the contacts between the foster family and biological family members of the foster child were merely tolerated for the sake of the foster child. It was not only on ideological grounds that most foster mothers did not want contact with the biological parents; many foster mothers also experienced an increased workload after the foster children had been visiting their parents. The foster mothers felt that in many cases they had to spend a lot of time "picking up the pieces" after visits.

Many foster mothers rejected outright the forced role of mediating between the foster child and his/her parents. They felt that the foster child's parents were the responsibility of the state/social worker. The foster mothers who did have contact with the foster child's parents were often frustrated. One foster mother explained her frustration:

> When they [foster children] went back to the mom, she asked me their bedtimes and what they liked to eat and what they did do for activities and what their hobbies and stuff were and how they were doing in school and stuff. None of that was applied apparently, when they went back, because when they came back the second time [in foster care], they did whatever they pleased.... No, I would rather that there wasn't any contact. It really again de-

pends on circumstances because some natural parents can be very violent (1247).

The foster mothers seemed to feel that they failed the child when they had any extended contact with the foster child's family. In fact, foster mothers were caught in a quandary. They clearly did not like to have contact with the biological parents. On the other hand, they were keenly aware that no matter what the child's background, the child's parents were important to the child and eventually most foster children will return to the biological parents. At best, the relationship between the foster mothers and the foster child's parents was uncomfortable, emotional and rocky; at worst, it was hostile.

Under the current construction of foster care, foster mothers in this study reported that they would like to have as little contact with the foster child's parents and family as possible because foster mothers felt that contact was most often unsatisfactory. Foster mothers felt little sympathy for the biological parents, and were insistent that the parents should "shape up" and become good parents, even though they recognized that there was little support within the system to help them. Moreover, some foster mothers felt that their safety, the safety of their family and the safety of the foster child were put at risk when the foster child's parents knew too much about them. Given their explicit notions about mothering as "an automatic skill," foster mothers were pessimistic that biological parents could change their parenting behaviour.

Foster mothers wanted to take care of other women's children because they wanted to mother them. As a result, they wanted little contact with the children's biological mother, choosing instead to regard her as a failed mother for whom there was little hope of change. Furthermore, foster mothers experienced what they perceived to be the results of failed parenting, both in terms of the multi-faceted problems which characterized many foster children and the dashed hopes after unsuccessful visits with the biological family. When this happened the foster mothers had to deal with the fallout: a hurt and embittered child. Foster mothers clung rather tightly to their attitudes about the biological parents of foster children because these views were so often reinforced by unsuccessful home visits.

THE PARADOX

Foster mothers were very reluctant to interpret their care as anything other than mother care. This should not be a surprise considering the fact that the state augments this view foster mothers have of themselves. They are scrutinized and investigated by the official representatives of the state to be certified "good" mothers, while the foster child is "rescued" by the same agency from a "failed" mother. Swift argues that:

> When children are removed from the care of their mothers, the proposed remedy is the "rescue" of the children from the mother, usually leading to the substitution of another mother for the original deficient mother. That the work and responsibility is passed on to another woman is seldom questioned. (1991:261)

Much of the difficulty foster mothers experience with the notion of increased responsibility for contact with the child's biological family is linked to their perception of their own role as foster mother. As long as these women see themselves as the mother who rescues the foster child and provides that child with mother love and mother care, family reunification will appear to undermine both the role and purpose of the foster mother. Because the care of foster mothers is rooted in mothering skills, which are believed to be within the repertoire of every woman who bears a child, it is no accident that these women are very reluctant to interact with the "other" mother. Without a doubt, the reluctance of the foster mother to have contact with the foster child's biological mother is in large measure a result of the conflict of the two mothering roles: the "good" versus the "bad" mother. Nevertheless, foster mothers reported that they complied with the request to have contact with the natural parents because the social worker who makes the request also has the power to remove the foster child.

While the ideology of mothering held by foster mothers may appear to challenge emerging social-work notions about the importance of family reunification (Maluccio et al. 1993), the state has fostered this ideology by seeking out a pool of women who are willing to care for other women's children without receiving any wages for their labour. The fact that foster-care providers see their caring as an extension of their mothering explains why women are willing to foster with no financial rewards for their work.

NOTES

1. However, mandatory provisions of child protection apply only to children sixteen years and younger.
2. Several provinces have separate foster-care programs for Native children's welfare. In some Western Provinces, Native child welfare programs are part of the regular child welfare programs with separate Native departments. This study does not include any data on Native child welfare programs.
3. It is not known how long these children remained with their biological families (Smith 1991:177). Other studies have indicated that children in foster care who are not able to stay in contact with their natural parents fare poorly (Berridge and Clever 1987; Steinhauer 1991). Many foster-care agencies advocate the involvement of biological parents. Nevertheless, in practice, few resources are placed in the programs to make the biological parents' involvement successful (Galaway et al. 1994). "The actual practice of birth parents' participation is substantially less than agency policy would indicate" (80). A number of reasons can be identified to explain the gap between policy and practice. The authors speculate that biological involvement is not always in the best interest of the child and that perhaps some logistics like geography may hinder contact.
4. Kufeldt does not suggest that biological parents should be involved at all costs. Sometimes face-to-face contact between foster children and their parents may be "contra indicated" (1994:92).
5. The process is the same for foster mothers and fathers; because my study examined the lives of foster mothers, I will use the term foster mother throughout.

Chapter 3

Foster Mothers and Foster Children

THE CENTRAL RELATIONSHIP

The central relationship in foster care is the relationship be tween the foster mother and the foster child. This relationship is complex, unequal and asymmetrical. One can argue that a relationship between an adult and a child is always unequal in terms of power; however, the relationship between a foster mother and a foster child is not only unequal, it encompasses several layers of additional complexities. For example, foster mothers have the power to "return" foster children to the agency when the relationship does not work out; foster children do not have this power. The asymmetry in the relationship is rooted in the fact that a foster mother chooses to take care of foster children, while foster children hardly every choose to be taken care of by a foster mother. The relationship lacks the taken-for-grantedness which is present in a regular mother–child relationship. It is characterized by formal conditions and parameters.

The foster mothers who participated in this study were poignantly aware of the difficult conditions that characterized the foster child–foster mother relationship. As a result, they developed a number of strategies to facilitate the foster child's transition to a foster home. Their goal was to make the child's entry into the foster family as easy and as pleasant as possible. Nevertheless, as soon as a foster child entered a foster family, dramatic changes in the familial dynamics occurred and these changes affected the entire family.

ARRIVAL

Foster mothers usually had little time to prepare for the arrival of a foster child. In some instances the foster child arrived half an hour after the foster mother received a call from a social worker concerning a placement. In other cases it took up to a week before the foster child arrived. Sometimes the foster mother was asked to pick up the child from the social worker's office or from a hospital; in other cases the social worker brought the child to the foster mother's home. In a few cases, the child came on his/her own to the foster home or was brought by a previous caregiver. As one foster mother explained:

> this fellow I got, now the worker did not come. He [foster child] asked to come here. My brother has a group home and he brought him in. I was lucky to get an outline [background information] from my brother. I mean they [social workers] never came at all. (1118)

Although there was often little time between the initial phone call and the arrival of the foster child, most foster mothers felt prepared because they saw this timing element as part of their commitment to fostering.

The major issue that foster mothers felt uncomfortable about was not the sudden arrival of the foster child, but the lack of what they called "background information." Foster mothers felt that they often did not receive enough background information about the foster child. The *Foster Homes Standards* (New Brunswick 1990a:5) manual states that "all foster parents have the right to full disclosure of pertinent information regarding a foster child." However, the foster mothers believed strongly that much of the information about the child's background is considered confidential information by social workers, who are not willing to disclose it. Many foster mothers did not object to the fact that some of the child's background could be withheld; they did feel that far too often information needed to care properly for the foster child was not provided. Foster mothers wanted information on mundane matters such as bedtime routines, the child's favourite foods etc.

The provision of important and pertinent background information is not only related to the feeling that "knowing a little bit more about the foster child" would improve the care; in some cases the lack of pertinent background information endangered the health of the foster child. For example, one foster mother was not made aware that her foster child had a serious congenital medical condition for which the child needed ongoing medical monitoring. Consequently the foster child did not receive special medical care when exposed to an intrusive medical treatment (dental work). Fortunately the dental work did not have any negative impact, but a simple infection resulting from a tooth extraction could have had serious consequences for the child's health. The foster mother stumbled by accident upon this knowledge when the foster child's grandmother mentioned in passing how pleased she was with the health of the "miracle baby." The foster mother explained:

> They do not want to give you a lot of information because it is not your right to know. But is it? I don't know? She [foster child's grandmother] told me one day on the phone about this miracle baby [the foster child] and that it was a miracle that he lived. That is how we found out.... [T]hey did not even know at the Children's Aid ... if they knew they did not tell us.... He never had check ups. He needed to be checked and re-checked; he needs to be watched, looked after. (1307)

Another foster mother gave different reasons why she would like to have more information on the background of a prospective foster child than the social workers volunteered. She wanted to assess whether the child would fit in her family. She described her motives:

> [They tell you] the child's name, this is how old he is, this is what time he is arriving at your house. Then you ask: "Can you tell me a little bit about him, what are his characteristics?" Then they will tell you, only then. Most of the time you know the age and name. I always feel bad like about asking what's the child like. It makes me feel as if I only want a good child but that is not what I want it to

sound. I want it to sound like I care what's coming into my home. I just wanted to know what to expect when he arrived. I don't need personal information. I don't care if I know where the child comes from; that's none of my business. But I do want to know if the child is afraid of the dark. If the child has dislikes? If he has allergies? Is he afraid of people? Is he a happy child? Is he a lonely child? Is it all right if he stays in his room all the time? Is that what he would normally do? Is he a loner? These little things, not what did his mother and father do to him, where does he come from. That is not the information I want. (1558)

It is not clear why foster mothers do not always receive pertinent background information. Some foster mothers believed that social workers did not provide them with more information because they themselves had little; others felt that in some cases the social worker did not tell the "whole story" for fear that the foster mother would not want the foster child. Even when a social worker did disclose pertinent information, many foster mothers felt that social workers tended to minimize the severity of the child's physical or behavioural problems so as to make the child more "placeable." The danger of this conduct, even though perhaps understandable from the perspective of social workers, is that the expectations of the foster mothers and the behaviour of the foster child may be incongruous, increasing the chance of foster placement breakdown, which in turn may be devastating to the wellbeing of the foster child. One foster mother recalled her experiences:

the social worker has only so much time, they never give you enough background.... When they are therapeutic, [a label for a foster child with special needs] ... they say it is just a normal child with a little problem in the house, then you get a record [background information] and then you find out that the child has a record that long, they don't tell you these things. If you knew, you would be a little bit more prepared for this stuff. I tell you if you are not a strong foster parent, you can break [down] a week after that child is in the house. (1209)

The lack of pertinent background information had a number of dangers attached to it. For example, regardless of the background information received by the foster mother, many foster children sooner or later disclosed some aspect of the abuse that had happened to them, usually when the child had reached a certain comfort level with the foster mother. The foster mother had no way of knowing whether this was previously disclosed abuse or abuse that the child had not revealed before. This placed her in a difficult position. Foster mothers have a duty to report to the state when a foster child discloses past abuse. Although this may be a good policy, some foster mothers felt that the law required them to "betray" the foster child's trust, particularly when the child wanted to disclose the abuse only to the foster mother and not to the social worker. When a social worker learns of abuse, she has an obligation to initiate an investigation, an event the foster child may not have wanted to precipitate. Foster mothers sometimes feel caught between the psychological needs of the foster child and their obligation to the child welfare services. If they reported the disclosed abuse, foster mothers felt that they betrayed the trust that had been so carefully built over time between them and their foster child. If they did not report the past abuse they were in violation of the state's policies.

THE STAY

Several foster mothers felt that girls were easier to handle, while others felt that boys were easier. Family make-up and the physical space of the foster family sometimes determined the gender of the foster child the foster family could care for. The gender stereotypes that permeate society were also part of the gender-typing by foster mothers. Some foster mothers found girls more emotional, less tidy around the home, messy and difficult when suffering from PMS. Boys were considered tougher and rougher although some foster mothers felt that boys showed them more respect than girls did. The gender preference in foster children by foster mothers was deeply rooted in their personal experience of raising their own children and their own gender-typing.

A common experience during the first part of the stay of the foster child in the foster family home was what foster mothers called "the honeymoon period." This is a period of time ranging from a couple of days to a few weeks when the foster child "tries to please you" and the foster family members try hard to get to know and to please the foster child and make the foster child "feel at home." This is the period during which the foster mother wondered what all the "fuss" was about if the foster child had been described as having behavioural problems. However, after the honeymoon period, the children start "testing you to see what your reaction is and whether or not you are going to send them to another home and these sort of things" (1135).

Foster mothers developed all kinds of skills and strategies to make the new foster child feel comfortable while they anxiously waited for the "true child" to emerge. Some foster mothers tried to make the child comfortable with his/her favourite foods. Others tried to comfort the child with talk. The first couple of days, and particularly nights, after the foster child arrived were often difficult, according to the foster mothers. Whatever the reasons why the foster child was apprehended and whatever the trauma the child had suffered, "the first thing at night is they all want their mommies" (1135).

One of the first tasks foster mothers undertook, particularly when the foster child was old enough to comprehend, was to instruct them in the house rules. Some foster mothers had the rules written down; others discussed them with the children. They all seemed to agree that it was important that the foster child learn to adhere to these rules. Some foster mothers gave the child a little bit of time to get used to the house rules; others enforced them from day one.

After the foster child had settled in and the entire family, including the foster child, was used to some new routines, one of the most intense aspects of fostering would occur. If the foster child and the foster family got along and developed a positive relationship, the foster placement could be seen as successful. In that case, the child would stay till the end of the predetermined time period—on average three to six months—as ordered by the courts, but possibly much longer, sometimes years depending on the circumstances. If, for some reason, the relationship between the foster child and the foster family was not positive, the foster placement was threatened by premature breakdown.

Many aspects of the development of a positive relationship

between the foster mother, the foster family and the foster child were rooted in the child's past. Foster children who had been abused would frequently display a typical behaviour pattern that had in some instances a severe impact on the familial relationships.[1] Most foster mothers felt that the way foster children behaved towards them and other family members revealed the type of abuse the foster child had suffered. For example, many physically or sexually abused children did not want to be touched or hugged. They seemed to be fearful of intimate human contact. Other children were aggressive and again others were withdrawn and timid. In some cases the foster children exhibited extreme fear when confronted with a particular environment, such as the dark, or certain objects, such as a belt. Again others were constantly deceptive, according to the foster mothers, and the foster mothers would characterize these children as "liars" and "difficult to handle children." The following story exemplifies the fear a foster child may develop for a particular object:

> This last foster son keeps asking my husband why he doesn't hit the children. He keeps coming up to us and he always says, "Why don't you get mad, how come you don't get mad?" "How come you don't hit me?" I said: "Are you allowed to hit me?" "Well no, you're my Mom." So I said: "Am I allowed to hit you?" It is as simple as that. To him it is very hard to understand how come there is no physical abuse. I don't know his background, I don't know what happened to him. From the way he talks, I can tell that he is petrified of men that wear belts. He always asks [husband]: "How come you don't wear a belt?" "That's cause you don't hit kids eh?" So definitely the background really has an effect.... I know that he has been through a lot ... and it definitely comes out. (1558)

Some foster children, who the foster mothers suspected of having been sexually abused, would display inappropriate sexualized behaviour that was disturbing and confusing to many members in the foster family. These foster children did not know the appropriate way of asking for affection. One foster mother explained:

my husband goes around without his shirt a lot, he always does, it is just something he always did. I found that she [foster child] was very affectionate, always wanting to sit on his knee, always getting close, taking his arm and always rubbing him. It bothered [husband] and I. We watched it. She always wanted to kiss [husband]. She really had a fascination for [son] I found. That really bothered me so we talked to the Department about it and we had her checked out. She was looking for affection in the wrong way. It just seemed like with the men, like if [son] would get up in the morning with his pajamas on and no top, it was just like she ... I don't know what it was. Maybe it was nothing, I don't know. Nothing ever came out of it, it just stopped.... She started wanting to kiss on the lips ... no matter what, always wanted to. I figured that there was something like that probably ... but that stopped completely. We just watch and we talked to [son]. [We told him]: "When you are around [foster child], you make sure that you are fully covered." He does. He got angry with me the first time, he couldn't understand why, after we explained it to him he did. (1535)

The foster child's previous abuse and the resulting behaviour sometimes had a tremendous impact on the relationships between the foster family members and the foster child, as well as among the foster family members themselves. One of the worrisome issues for some foster families, in particular when the foster child asked for affection in a sexual manner, was the fear of being accused of physical or sexual misconduct. In particular, foster fathers were very reserved in dealing with foster children who displayed sexualized behaviour. Four foster mothers talked explicitly about the fear of "false allegations" although none of the foster mothers interviewed had ever been accused of sexually abusing foster children. The foster mothers knew that the foster children needed healthy affection, but if the foster child was not able to ask for non-sexual affection the giving of healthy affection to the child by foster family members became problematic.

Moving On

Although there are other reasons why foster children leave foster families, e.g., adoption, independent living for teenagers and moves to other foster homes, the most important reason why foster children leave the foster family is to be returned to their biological parents. No matter what the reasons for departure, foster mothers typically felt saddened and worried about the foster child even though they knew "the idea of fostering [is] to go back to their natural parents" (1220). In a few cases the foster mothers were relieved when the child left, but the majority of the foster mothers stated that letting the foster children go was the most difficult aspect of fostering. "It is easier to take them in than to let them go" (1320) was a very common sentiment.

In general, the foster mothers felt that there was enough time to prepare the foster child and themselves for the departure. In the case of a fixed period of caring ordered by the courts, the date of departure could be anticipated far in advance. However, sometimes a foster mother would get a call and had only one day or a few days to prepare the child and herself for the impending departure. When this happened, foster mothers felt that the departure of the foster child was very difficult emotionally, not only for them, but also for the child.

The reason for departure of the foster child often set the mood for how the foster mother felt towards the issue of "moving on." When the child went back to the same, unchanged, biological home environment, the foster mothers felt sad and angry. They felt that "all their work had been for nothing." As one foster mother described it: "I do not like any of my children to go. I get upset with every child that leaves, particularly when they go back to the same environment and nothing has improved" (1095). Another foster mother described the leaving process as follows:

> Sometimes we know that our time has come up for six months. Say, for instance, it was coming up, we sort of prepare ourselves mentally for that. The social worker will have more visits with us. So we slowly pack things, slowly talk to them and tell them that they are going to go back. Most cases we have had, they were not ready to go back [but] whether they think they are or not they go

anyway. It's awful hard when that day actually comes. [Husband] and I never handle that very well. We never say goodbye, we always say we'll see you later. (1535)

Some foster mothers felt that social workers involved them in the leaving of the foster child, but many felt that they were not consulted or involved in the leaving process except to pack the bag and get the foster child ready. In fact, the majority of foster mothers believed that the foster child was not ready to leave. Some felt that the foster child's family was not ready to care for the child again. The ultimate decision about the foster child leaving was made by the courts or the social worker; the foster mothers had no formal say in that process.

One foster mother refused to take part in the leaving process of her foster child, because she was absolutely convinced that the biological mother was not ready to take care of the child. She explained:

> they called, they said: "Can you have [G] ready for Friday." I said: "You must have the wrong child." "No" she said. So I wondered where she was going. They said that she was going back to her mother. There was no court hearing. I prepared her and made her ready but I refused to take her. I refused to be part of it. (1133)

Another foster mother felt:

> When they go to a good situation I can get happy for that person. I can let go, but when they go to a place like [biological parents] you never forget that. You always wonder. I think we should have more input than we do. (1135)

Another foster mother talks about "withdrawal" symptoms when a foster child moves on. She explained:

> [Husband] and I go through a withdrawal for a good week or more, like there is just a part of us that they took from us.... I think about the kids a lot, wondering what

they are doing. But then they [Department of Health and Community Services] must have known what they were doing when they took them back. (1535)

Foster mothers unanimously agreed that they wanted to stay in touch with the foster children after they left their care. In many instances that did happen, particularly for older children, because these children initiated the contact themselves and foster mothers encouraged their ex-foster children to call collect. In the case of younger children, the foster mothers needed cooperation from the Department of Health and Community Services or the next set of caregivers. Foster mothers felt strongly that the Department of Health and Community Services did not facilitate contact between the foster mothers and the departed foster children. They seemed to adhere to the notion that the foster mother's role is really temporary and is finished and should be completely terminated as soon as the child leaves. Some adoptive parents also felt that the foster parents should not be allowed to stay in touch with the foster child.

Thus for foster mothers, in particular of younger children, it was often not possible to remain in contact with the foster child they had cared for. Foster mothers found this hard to accept. One foster mother looked after a young foster child who was eventually adopted. She has never heard from the child again; she likened that feeling to having somebody die:

> he went for adoption and we never knew where he went and we have never seen him again. It is almost death to us. (1135)

However, some foster mothers, in particular the women who cared for older children, remained important confidantes in the lives of their departed foster children. One foster mother tells her story:

> They always call and I've had them even come visit us, or we have stopped and picked them up and took them to the playground for ice-cream. A lot of times we meet them in the stores and they get so excited to meet you and

it is great, it is a real good feeling like that. (1535)

The foster mothers felt that the state did not recognize the importance of the child's ties with the foster family. The state seemed, according to the foster mothers, to want to ignore or eradicate the time the child had spent in foster care. This attitude is difficult to accept for the foster mothers. They have invested time and physical and emotional energy in a foster child and suddenly they have to let go and are not able to remain in occasional contact. As a result, foster mothers were unanimous in describing the leaving process as the most difficult aspect of their relationship with the foster children.

TESTIFYING IN COURT

Foster mothers expressed a lot of discomfort with the fact that they sometimes were called upon to testify in court on behalf of the Department of Health of Community Services. The reason for their testimony was mostly in respect to the discontinuation of the parental rights of the biological parents. The court brought one foster mother face to face with the biological parent. Her identity, as well as the place where she lived, were revealed. She argued:

> I have kind of mixed feelings about that. But if that is the way it has to be, it has to be. They would know where we live and everything because you have to state where you live and all that. (1247)

Foster mothers do not like to confront biological parents and prefer to keep contact with them to a minimum because foster mothers feel that they are the advocates solely for the mistreated child. They believe their role is to help the foster child and that social workers are responsible for helping the foster child's natural family.

Unconditional Love

Regardless of some of the behaviour of the foster children and the foster mothers' feelings towards the biological parents, many foster mothers demonstrated "unconditional" love toward their foster children (Reddy et al. 1994). For example, two foster mothers had adopted the handicapped children they were caring for because they feared for the children's future if they did not adopt them. Another foster mother had to deal with a deliberately set fire. She believed that the foster child had not intended to burn the house down; the child was merely asking for attention. However, the fire was sizeable and created a fair bit of damage. The foster mother explained her feelings and her decision to take the foster child back:

> We had a fire in the house and it was put on by the foster child.... After that we have always been scared. Like the gun and the knife we had to put that away in our bedroom. We always have that in the back of our mind. I have seen many times that when we go to bed, I have left the door open a little bit and then I think, somebody will come in here. You think that way before you go to bed, it is hard on the nerves. Sometimes it may cause problems for sleeping and that.... We had to let go of [the foster child] for while ... I was burned out. We had to let go the child but we took her back.... We find that we have put so much time, so many years in her life that we did not want to let her leave like that, we wanted do something more ... until the age when she is old enough to be by herself and maybe what we taught her will stay in her head. (1591)

Foster Care Breakdowns

When the foster mothers were asked whether they had cared for foster children that did not fit with their families, the initial response was negative. However, soon after making this reply, many foster mothers remembered one or two placements that did not work out and where they had to ask the social worker to remove the foster child from the family. The foster child could have been a preschooler or a teenager. One foster mother's narrative was as follows:

> Almost all of them have fit. It has worked out, in fact there have been people would say: "Look, you would say that is your [own] child." ... I try to think back, I can only think of one that did not fit. He did not fit, he did not have the same morals and he did not want our morals pushed on him. He was very blunt about it. But he had problems. He did not want us to help him. He really was not a part of our family, and he never felt part of this family and we never felt that he was part of the family. That was the one child that I have asked to be removed. (1133)

Another foster mother described her experiences with a pre-teen:

> He was twelve years old and he had been into a number of foster homes, he was going to go into a reformatory when he left here, we were told ... It didn't work. He was a runaway and every time he took off I was scared to death that something would happen [to him] on this road. He wanted to be with his mother. His mother would call me up and tell me to come and get him and that hurt worse than anything. He just got too much for me and I just said that's it, I can't take it. Because, I am not going to be responsible if he gets picked up by somebody on the road or gets killed. I found it too hard with my [own] young fellow. (1220)

One foster mother could not handle two little boys and asked the social worker to remove them. She explained:

> They threw rocks at me, they threw rocks at the patio door, they spit at me, they scratched me, they kicked me.... [Husband] said, "I am not going to work and leave these kids with you." So I called the Department and said: "I just can not handle this." While I was waiting for [another] foster Mom to pick them up, I had to sit in a chair and hold one child because he was [trying] to go in

my bathroom and wreck it. I had to sit with him and hold him tight. Every time I had to let him go he bolted down the hall and got in the bathroom. It was not worth it. (1135)

It was intriguing that the foster mothers initially denied having "sent" a foster child back. When a foster placement does not work out, the foster mother often blames herself, instead of the structures under which foster care is administered, and she has to counter or even change her self-image from a successful mother to a failed mother. It is no wonder that foster mothers did not readily want to talk about, or had forgotten, the unsuccessful foster placements.

NOTE

1. Not all children in foster care have been physically or sexually abused—neglect and abandonment are the most frequent causes for state family interventions.

Chapter 4

Foster Mothers,
their Families and Others

The foster family is a paradoxical institution. In order to care for traumatized children, many foster families, and in particular foster mothers, make financial and other sacrifices However, the majority of the foster mothers surveyed for this study, 88 percent, also cared for their own children. Thus, in order to care for foster children, the foster families' own children often had to sacrifice time and financial resources. The patterns of intense caring that were required by many foster children had a profound impact on the foster mother's own familial relationships. Furthermore, these patterns of intense caring also affected the foster mother's job performance. As a result, fostering is much more than a relationship between the foster child, the foster mother and the state. In fact the entire family, members of the extended family and co-workers (willingly or unwillingly) are also affected by the fostering work of foster mothers.

FOSTER MOTHERS AND PAID WORK

Almost half of the foster mothers surveyed for this study did not work for pay outside the home (54 percent); the other half of the foster mothers had full-time (27 percent) or part-time (19 percent) work outside the home. The impact of fostering on the foster mother who worked for pay outside the home was considerable, often interfering with her paid work. This interference was frequently related to crisis situations that seemed to mark the lives of many, in particular older, foster children. School teachers and/

or principals called foster mothers when a foster child's behaviour caused problems in the school, and police officers called foster mothers when the child's behaviour caused problems in public places. It was expected that foster mothers would immediately respond to the crisis, taking time off work if necessary. For example, one foster mother was shopping in a large department store when her name was announced over the public announcement system. She had to go to the phone in order to deal with a crisis involving her two teenage foster daughters. Fostering is not a private activity; it very much penetrates the public and workplaces of the foster mothers.

Sometimes the workplace of the foster father was also affected. Stay-at-home foster mothers occasionally called their husbands at work to respond to a crisis around the foster child at home or at school. In one instance, the foster child "got out of hand" at home and the foster mother was not able to handle it. She called her husband and demanded that he come home immediately to help deal with the crisis. Although the demands on working mothers to combine work and family responsibilities are well-known (Hochschild 1989), the demands on working foster mothers are heightened because of the intense caring necessary for youth with behavioural problems.

For some foster mothers the demands of work and fostering were not compatible, and they decided to terminate their paid employment in order to better care for a foster child. One foster mother resigned her job so she could care for five small foster children, all siblings. She described the process of getting them:

> I asked for time to discuss [the placement of five small children] with my husband, with the children that were already here and with the family. But there was no time, this was an emergency sort of thing and they said that they would bring them here just overnight until they got another place. But I couldn't have that, I wouldn't bring five little children into one strange place and then zap them out the next day to another strange place, I couldn't handle that so I automatically, right off the top of my head thought, well I think we can do it. We'll give it a big try.... I said okay, and within an hour they were here. Within

that hour I had a chance to talk to [husband]. He was bewildered and angry. So I said well they are coming and I said if you don't want them here tomorrow they can be removed, taken to another home, if you feel that you can let this happen after meeting these kids, I'll go along with it because I don't want to upset things.... They stayed for a year. So, we handled it. For three months, it was hell. Now today I miss them dearly, terribly, I should say. I stopped my job. There was no way with the real tiny one. I think she was two months, well going on pretty well three months. The second one was eighteen months and then three, four and five. I felt they needed me, I needed my job badly but my job could wait. I only thought it was going to be for a short time but as time went on, it was a year. It was quite a struggle without that job but it was good, it paid off. (1320)

After the foster children left, she went back to her old job.

Foster mothers who worked outside the home were by and large employed in the service industry (short order cook, supermarket bakery, etc.) Given that many of these families could use the additional income, the most significant aspect of giving up the job was the loss of that income. Although foster mothers received "room and board" from the state as a compensation for cost of caring, the cost of caring for foster children outweighed the compensation.

In some cases, foster family members pressured the foster mother to quit the paying job so that she could spend more time at home. One foster mother who cared for three foster children (siblings) was considering quitting her job at the time of the interview. Although she herself was reluctant to stop working for pay, her husband felt she should stay home because of the increased workload due to the care of the children. Thus, sometimes foster mothers were urged by other family members into decisions concerning paid work that they themselves did not wholeheartedly support.

A foster mother who had quit her job in order to look after a foster child explained:

Nobody will babysit this one. My son does the babysitting. I had a full-time job and I cut it down to two days a week because of my foster son, it was just impossible. Now this is my last week, I gave my two weeks notice and now I am completely finished work. I had to choose what was more important in life: helping a child out or making a few extra dollars. So I think the former won out. I worked in a men's clothing store and I really enjoyed my job but I think this is more important because everybody has given up on him and I am afraid that if I give up on him too, it's just one more on the list; it's just he needs a push and this is a main push I think. So it is all right, I will get another job but I'll never get another [S] if I let him go. I'll never get the chance that I have now, whereas work I can have another chance at it. (1558)

This foster mother felt strongly that her work with the foster child was more important than her paid employment, and she also felt that if this foster placement broke down, the foster child would be set on the course of a very unhappy and troubled adult life. She chose the wellbeing of the foster child over her own desire to work as a sales clerk.

Two of the twenty foster mothers who were interviewed had terminated their employment in order to give full attention to their foster children. They did not see this as a sacrifice; they felt strongly that the children would not do well without full-time mothering. We can conclude that fostering severely impacted on the paid work activities of the foster mothers. They either had to be stay-at-home mothers or they had to be willing to put up with work interruptions, sometimes severe ones.

THE CHILDREN OF THE FOSTER FAMILY

Not all foster families had their own children, or if they did, sometimes these children were adults and no longer lived at home. However, foster mothers who had their own children living at home reported that their own children sometimes felt neglected or jealous of the attention the foster children received. As one foster mother described it:

> The kids have to make an adjustment to a new child
> coming in. They tend to be a little jealous at times, particu-
> larly when I have a child in here that I have to spend a
> great deal of time with. They tend to feel a little neglected.
> Even though I am not. You have to kinda find a balance
> you know. Sometimes it is tough. (1188)

Sometimes the foster mother's biological children had to lock
up their belongings for fear of theft. In one case the adult daughter put a lock on her bedroom door. Another area that created
difficulties between biological children and foster children was
the clothing allowances. Although foster children did not get a lot
of money to clothe themselves, they usually got it in a lump sum.
Most foster children would spend the lump sum all at once,
leaving a foster mother's biological children jealous because the
foster mothers were not always in a position to spend that much
money in one shopping spree on their biological children. One
foster mother reported:

> foster kids were expected to be dressed very well ... for
> our kids, we could not afford to do that. So, of course that
> was one of the things that a couple of times they would
> come out and say: "How come so and so can have brand
> new jeans and we don't?" (1133)

However, most foster mothers felt strongly that fostering had
few negative effects on their own children. The overwhelming
sense of the foster mothers was that their biological children
benefited tremendously from being in a foster family. The biggest
benefits for their biological children were believed to be that they
learned to share materially and emotionally with less fortunate
people and therefore to value their home environment instead of
taking it for granted. Also a number of foster mothers reported
that when their biological children noticed what drugs and "hanging out with the wrong crowd" did to foster children's lives, it
was a potent reminder not to get involved in these situations.
One foster mother explained:

> it is kind of a teaching process for them [biological chil-

dren] too. They see the children, these young teenagers [foster children] either on drugs, alcohol, you name it…. My son has commented to me, he goes: "Wow Mom, I don't think I'd ever want to get mixed up like that on drugs or alcohol or anything like that." So it is a teaching process too. But at the same time, depending on what the background of the teenager is and what they may have done as a young offender, you sort of have to keep an extra eye out for my own children's safety and what not. (1157)

Although fostering was very time consuming and there were some negative effects, most foster mothers felt that the positive aspects of fostering on their own children outweighed the negative. This conclusion is not surprising considering the fact that foster mothers' care is rooted in mothering. Foster mothers perceive themselves to be "good" mothers. Therefore, they would not easily admit that fostering may be an activity that would jeopardize the "good" mothering of their own children.

The Spousal Relationship

Of the twenty foster mothers interviewed, one was divorced and one widowed; the rest were married at the time of the interview. Although foster mothers felt they needed the support of their spouses, it was the foster mothers who did most of the caring. The foster father played an important and yet a marginalized role. Most foster mothers felt that they needed the support from their spouses and that fostering without that support would be impossible. At the same time, the foster father rarely looked after the foster child on a day-to-day basis. In some cases, he would do some fun things with the kids such as playing games or taking them to the ballpark, or he might be called upon to establish order when a foster child was out of control. One foster mother explained:

I'm the disciplinarian: "Go and ask Mommy, it is up to Mom." I say, I am tired of looking like the bad guy here and he'd say: "Well somebody has got to be the good guy." But like, he is the one that will take them to the concerts and stuff like that…. He plays hockey with them, he plays ball and all this, but I do all the other stuff, the girlie, the shopping. (1047)

The most often reported negative impacts of fostering on the spousal relationship were the lack of privacy and the lack of time. As one foster mother noted, there was "less time to be together." The lack of privacy related to intimate relationships as well as all other aspects of the foster family's affairs. One foster mother stated:

> you really don't have privacy. We kinda geared our lives to it. At first, the foster kids that lived with us knew what our hydro bills were, phone bills were. When we bought a new car [they knew] basically how much we paid for the car. Then they would tell everybody. (1071)

The lack of privacy was an aspect of fostering that the foster mothers did not like and had not anticipated. Privacy could be created by using relief weekend foster families or babysitters, the cost of which the state will reimburse. However, money for babysitters was not the major issue; the major problem was the inability to find babysitters or substitute weekend relief foster parents who were willing to look after the foster children. As a result some foster mothers felt "tied down." When foster mothers were taking care of teenage children the problem was less acute than when the foster children were young. One foster mother who cared for three young children commented:

> I cannot find a babysitter. Nobody will look after them. They do it once and that is game over. I cannot find anybody. So we are stuck seven days a week, twenty-fours hours a day. (1307)

The lack of privacy, was considered one of the major issues that impacted on the spousal relationship and could not be easily resolved. In many cases the teenage or mature biological children of the foster mother would babysit when needed, but foster mothers who did not have this support had few opportunities to "take a break." This in turn could lead sometimes to tension between the foster mother and her partner and/or other family members. One foster mother stated that every time the family has a new foster child placed with them, it creates tension in her relationship with her spouse:

> There is tension at times, we fight. When you have new children in the home ... we don't know how each [of us] feels about it until we get into it a bit. This causes a lot of tension at times. (1535)

Although foster mothers had not anticipated the difficulties, disruptions and lack of privacy when they started caring for foster children, they felt that fostering had by and large a positive influence on their own children and their spouses.

THE EXTENDED FAMILY, FRIENDS AND OTHERS

Becoming a foster family not only changed the relationships within the immediate family, it also meant that new or changing affiliations occurred with other people outside the family. When a foster child moved in, the child brought with him/her at least a social worker and sometimes many more professional caregivers or therapists, people the foster family did not have contact with before they entered fostering. The existing relationships among the foster family, the extended family, professionals and neighbours sometimes changed.

Many foster mothers mentioned that their own extended families were reluctant to support their fostering. In some cases, the extended family was concerned about the impact of fostering: i.e., the foster mother had less time for the extended family because of the increased workload. For example, a foster mother described her own mother's attitude as follows: she "always thinks I am running myself down" (1535). In other cases, the extended family members felt that it was often too difficult for the foster mother to say goodbye to the foster child creating emotional distress for her which in turn impacted on the extended family. One foster mother described her extended family's response to her fostering as follows:

I can't say that they truly understand. I think after twenty years they are coming to grips with it in my family but they don't understand it.... you can't always be with the family, other things supersede when you are doing this [fostering]. And they also see you hurting when the children leave so of course because they love you they can't understand why. They also get involved in the children's lives so it was a hurt for them too. If I didn't do this then they would not have to go through that either. No, they don't always understand. (1167)

Some other foster mothers' families did not express hesitation concerning fostering and were very supportive and "love[d] it." "My mother would say: 'Ah, you got a new one? Bring them up, I want to see them'" (1639).

Some people outside the extended family reacted positively when they found out that a woman was a foster parent, while others were negative:

[Some say] "It must be a wonderful experience?" or "What a wonderful person you are!" and on and on. [Others say] "I don't know how you can do that." I never know whether to be insulted or complimented. (1167)

Another foster mother, who provided childcare in her home, found that the parents of the daycare children removed their children from her care because "the foster children would be a bad influence on the children" (1095).

Although teachers, doctors and therapists did not always see the foster mother as the advocate and "mother" of the foster child, the foster mothers saw themselves in this way. One foster mother explained her feelings:

I am the mother. Don't treat my kids bad because I will fight for them. The school ... well they know me. I have volunteered a lot at the school so they all know me and they call. I have no problems ... they check things out with me. They do not call the Department [of Health and Community Services] they call me. I'm mom. (1047)

Another foster mother said that when she went to the school of her foster children to speak to the teacher, she made a point to talk about "my children" (1320). Some foster mothers reported that when they took their foster children in for medical exams the foster mother was not told what was going on because of the "confidential nature" of information concerning a foster child. They cared for the child twenty-four hours a day and did not appreciate this attitude. Some felt that, as a result, the foster children received inappropriate or improper medical care.

One foster mother, who insisted that there was "something wrong with the child" (infant), felt that she had to fight hard and take a lot of initiative to get the medical establishment to take care of the child. According to her, the state also did not take her concerns seriously. She felt that the state wanted to place the child as a "healthy newborn" and therefore was not too interested in pursuing her contention "that there was something wrong" with the child.

SUPPORT SERVICES

Although the foster mothers were aware that the state provided support services for foster families, most of these services were specifically geared towards the foster child. In fact, foster mothers have few people they can turn to for help. Because of the sensitive nature of their work and the promise of confidentiality concerning the foster child, many foster mothers turned to other foster parents for support. The formation of the New Brunswick Foster Parents Association was welcomed by many foster mothers.

Some foster mothers who did draw upon state support services, such as counsellors, psychologists, support workers (for special needs children) and foster-care workers, felt that the support they received was adequate. However, the majority stated that when they began to foster, nobody informed them about the availability of additional support services. Many foster mothers learned about these services by accident long after they began fostering, from other foster parents. Hence, many foster mothers severely resented the fact that the social workers did not bother to inform them about the available support services (such as relief care for weekends, daycare services for the child, or respite care in the case of special needs children) that could be accessed through the state. In addition they all felt that when they needed a social worker, s/he was never available. Appointments could be made two to three weeks in advance; however, in many cases the foster mother, when she did call a social worker, needed one instantly to deal with or to avert a crisis.

Some foster mothers had used support workers (paid helpers) because they cared for handicapped children who needed much attention, but their feelings were mixed about the usefulness of these services. Two foster mothers felt that the support workers actually increased their workload. One foster mother complained that because of the involvement of the support worker, she had to attend more meetings and explain to the support worker everything that needed to be done to properly care for the handicapped child. Another foster mother also had negative experiences with a support worker. She stated that the support worker was treating her unfairly, while "she got paid a lot more than me" (1133). By contrast, another foster mother who once had a support worker thought it was "very helpful" (1157).

Chapter 5

Foster Mothers and the State

The stories of the foster mothers revealed complex sets of relationships with a variety of people who play a role in foster-care delivery services. The complexity of these relationships arises from a number of conditions. First, the relationships among the people involved often go beyond formal responsibilities because the central person is a vulnerable child, evoking strong emotions in all. Second, the conduct of the various people in foster-care services is structured along bureaucratic lines and conditions as set out by the state. Third, there are dichotomies between paid workers such as social workers and therapists and unpaid foster mothers, and between the legal guardian—the state—and the day-to-day caregiver—the foster mother. The foster child brings a number of caregivers, such as therapists, doctors and psychologists, who encroach on the foster family. The foster family, and in particular the foster mother, become publicly scrutinized.

Foster mothers and their adult family members are assessed to determine whether they are suitable. A home study is undertaken, and a criminal record check on adults older than eighteen years of age living in the family is carried out. The state is allowed (with prior approval) to ask for medical and financial records from the various appropriate government departments. The developing relationship between the state and the foster mothers is, often to the surprise of the foster mothers, a very intrusive and intense one.

THE FILE

Once a family has been approved to be a foster family, the relationship between the state and the foster family intensifies dramatically. One aspect of the scrutiny foster families undergo is the compilation of a formal file containing up-to-date information regarding them. If the foster family experiences major changes, i.e., the addition of another child, financial changes or a planned move, they have to notify the state. The file contains the application form, references and health statement, the home assessment report, a copy of a letter of approval or rejection, a copy of the Foster Family Resource Agreement, a copy of every review and training record (*Foster Home Standards* 1990, s. 5-2). Furthermore, documents related to any recording by any worker "concerning the foster family's experiences" or complaints or investigations, are contained in the file. Foster families "shall have access, on request, to the information in the file" (*Foster Home Standards* 1990, s. 5-2). The official reason for the collection of this information is to safeguard the foster child's wellbeing. However, in the process, the foster family agrees to a severe degree of state intrusion into their day-to-day activities.

The state and child welfare agencies, however, are large amorphous bodies. The person who most often personifies the amorphous government body to the foster parents is a social worker. The first person women encounter when they become interested in fostering is the foster home worker, a qualified social worker "responsible for the provision of foster home services in their regions." Some of the responsibilities of this worker are to recruit, assess and approve foster homes, select the best placement for the foster children, ensure that the foster family is aware of the support services, oversee the effectiveness of the foster family and ensure that complaints by or against the foster family are investigated (*Foster Home Standards* 1990, s. 5-1).

Although the foster home worker assists foster families, his/her primary responsibility is towards the foster child. The fact that a foster home worker is responsible for carrying out an investigation when a complaint is launched against the foster family, demonstrates that families, in reality, do not have advocates to protect their interest in the foster-care services delivery system.

THE (LACK OF) SUPPORT IN THE SYSTEM

The relationship between foster mothers and the state is complex and this relationship is further complicated by the personal relationship that develops between the foster mother and the most important representative of the state, the social worker. The social worker's primary responsibility is towards the foster child, not the foster family. The foster mother's first contact may be the foster home worker; however, as soon as she is accepted and is ready to take a foster child in her home, she will have many more dealings with the foster child's social worker.

Foster mothers expressed ambivalent feelings towards social workers: on the one hand, social workers can be very helpful, but on the other hand, they can be very imposing and a source of conflict. The next story exemplifies these ambivalent feelings. The foster mother, who had fostered for many years, was accused by the mother of a foster child (that had left her care more than four years before) of physical abuse. The allegations of abuse were delivered on a Saturday morning by RCMP officers. The foster mother, because of the weekend, had no access to a social worker. She explains:

> we felt very alone when it happened, it was very inappropriate the way they [the Department of Health and Community Services] handled it in the beginning ... it happened on a Saturday morning. The RCMP came to the door and we had nobody to talk to all weekend. We did not know who we dared to speak to and we were frightened to tell anyone. We don't really know what happened.... Every time the phone rang we would jump and think that they would come and take our kids [foster and biological]. That is what is supposed to be done right away. Until we are proven innocent, they have to take all our kids.... [It took] six months; but your life is on hold for that period [before the allegations were proven unfounded].... That first weekend, I could visualize the house being gone, I thought this is going to be more than we can handle. We will not be able to afford the lawyer fees and the court fees. I was sure we were going to have to lose our house. (1133)

Only one social worker supported the foster parents through this ordeal. According to the foster mother, other social workers treated her and her family as if they were guilty of the alleged offence.

This story not only illustrates the lack of support for foster mothers, it also illustrates a very deeply felt resentment by foster mothers about the lack of advocates in the system for them. The social worker and the foster home worker's primary responsibilities are to the foster child. In general when foster mothers encounter allegations of maltreatment, little support is available (Carbino 1991). Carbino suggests that child welfare agencies should implement policies and support services for foster parents who have been alleged to have mistreated a foster child. The most important source of support for accused foster parents is often other foster parents.

THE RELATIONSHIP WITH SOCIAL WORKERS

Foster mothers care for foster children on a twenty-four-hour basis; nevertheless, important decisions concerning foster children's future are made by the bureaucracy with little or no input from the foster mothers. These women feel that social workers do not often view them as knowledgeable partners in foster-care services (Barter 1994). The experts are the social workers. One foster mother described her feelings:

> I would like to see the foster parents being more of a decision maker on behalf of the child instead of the social worker and the Department being totally in control. (1125)

Inexperienced social workers who impart academic knowledge to foster mothers without being able to understand their daily struggles prompted one foster mother to comment as follows:

> I don't know whose interest they are looking out for. I really don't know that! I'm really confused about Social Services Department. In my eyes I feel these social workers who have never done this, have no right to sit there and tell you how to do it. Yes, they have taken training for this, they have seen films and stuff like that but they

have not done the actual thing. That bothers me some-times when they can sit there and say you should be doing this, you should do that, or you have no right to do this. (1535)

Another foster mother stated:

Workers should be more mature. BSW should be a second degree. When you have workers twenty to twenty-one years old making decisions that are destroying children's lives; they have not got enough life experience to be given the power they have over families. (1243)

As illustrated above, the relationship between the foster moth-ers and the social workers is not always an easy one. Neverthe-less, foster mothers turn to social workers when they need help or in a crisis situation. However, besides their regularly scheduled appointments, it seemed almost impossible for foster mothers to get hold of the social workers. Needless to say, many foster mothers expressed severe frustration with the unavailability of the social worker when he or she was needed. One foster mother described her experiences:

There is just no getting hold of the people. They finally do get back to you and they say: "My case load is so booked, I cannot get back to you for another two weeks or so." Well, this child needs it now. "Well, I am sorry I cannot help you." (1639)

If a crisis arises the foster mother will have to deal with it herself without the support of the social worker, adding to her already very demanding schedule of day-to-day care of foster children. In addition, many foster mothers felt that social work-ers often did not inform them about additional support services such as relief care, babysitting services, daycare-fee reimburse-ment etc. Many foster mothers stated that they had to aggres-sively pursue these issues in order to get informed about the support services to which they were entitled. One foster mother commented that you can have access to support services "if you know who to ask and if you ask far enough in advance." Foster mothers were frustrated that they had to "fight for everything" (1209).

REIMBURSEMENT

The notion that foster mothers entered into fostering because of the money was a sore point for many, if not all, of the women interviewed. As indicated earlier, foster mothers do not get paid for their labour but receive compensation for the cost of caring for a foster child that ranges from $250 a month in New Brunswick to $800 a month in British Columbia. The feeling among foster mothers who received only $250 per month for "room and board" was that it was not enough to cover the actual cost. Many foster mothers in the study subsidized the foster child out of their own pockets. One foster mother described her feelings and the conflict that the inadequate reimbursement created in her family.

> I got $300 something for [foster child]. I could not keep my groceries in the house. And I bought a lot more groceries than his cheque was. You know ... so, I get $410. But still, a hundred dollars a week for a foster kid, you know, we used to get about $70 to $80 for groceries. Every night you have to go for milk. Really you don't make no money in foster care. If you are in it for the money, you would not be in it. (1118)

Foster mothers felt that, in general, they subsidize the foster children and they resent that others make the assumption that they foster for the money. Although most foster mothers did not like the fact that they had to subsidize the children, it was not a major issue for them.

Almost all foster mothers interviewed were adamant that they would not let the foster children suffer because the room and board fee was not adequate or the cheques did not come in time. One commented:

> A lot of times we don't even think of the money part. You just do it. If the child was with you, you don't say: "You do not have any money, you cannot come." Or we did not

get any money for you this week. We do not even look at it that way, we just go ahead and do it, we include them, money or no money (1157)

Others were more vocal about the fact that they had to subsidize the foster children. One foster mother felt that the biological parents should be held more responsible, particularly for future educational goals, for the child. She would like to adopt her teenage foster daughter; however, she also has a teenage son and she was not sure if she could afford to send both children to college. She felt strongly that the natural parents should be forced to contribute to an education fund for their children.

The fact that many foster mothers subsidized the foster children is the direct result of the fact that they view fostering as mothering, not as professional caregiving. Mothers do not get paid for their work; mothering is a "labour of love." Foster mothers have internalized this perspective in relation to the foster children, even though they provide twenty-four-hour care on behalf of the state.

THE PARADOX

One of the central paradoxes in foster care is how the state views the important service of child welfare. Children entering foster care have more severe problems than in the past, but the child welfare service in New Brunswick relies almost exclusively on women who volunteer their services to provide care and stability for children for whom the state acts as a guardian.[1]

A second paradox is that although the foster mothers care for the children around the clock, legally they are not the parent and therefore are often relegated to the fringes of important decisions affecting the foster child. The child is considered a ward of the state and the state "has full parental rights and shall exercise full parental responsibilities with respect to the child" (New Brunswick 1989: s. 3-2). Even though foster mothers care for the foster children "around the clock," it is the experts, the social workers, who are entrusted with the longterm planning for the child. This is a rather incoherent arrangement at best and precarious at worst for the foster child.

Interestingly, the state's advertisement paints a much more

sanguine picture of fostering in comparison to the experiences communicated by the foster mothers in this study. In fact the recruitment brochures use phrases such as: "No special skills required." The brochure goes on to state that "if you are able to love children you would make a good foster parent." No mention is made that foster children may have gone through a traumatic experience. There is only one explicit reference in the brochure that alludes to the problems foster mothers may encounter. In short, the state's recruiting literature for foster mothers does not reflect or provide any clues to the difficulties and tensions foster mothers encounter. This is not surprising considering the fact that the state has a difficult time attracting foster families and would not want potential applicants to be put off.

A third paradox lies in how foster mothers view their relationship with the state. This relationship is framed by a set of terms which are spelled out in the Foster Family Resource Agreement. However, not one foster mother in the interviews ever mentioned the existence of the Foster Family Resource Agreement or the fact that they had signed it. The Agreement "clearly indicates mutual expectations of both parties. The foster family shall be given a signed copy for their records" (New Brunswick 1990a: s. 2-10). Even though foster mothers sign a contract with the state, none of the foster mothers interviewed indicated that they saw their relationship with the state as a contractual one. They view fostering much more as a social responsibility. Only when they encountered difficulties with the foster children such that they requested that the foster children be removed, did they view their relationship more as a contractual one than one rooted in social responsibility.

The central paradox of the relationship between the state and foster mothers is beneficial to the state. If the state viewed foster-care services as professional care, just as the care social workers give is considered, they would be obliged to pay the foster mothers for their labour. As long as the state views foster care as an activity for which "no skills" are required, it can be presented as voluntary and there will not be any demand to pay the women who provide the care for foster children. Essential workers in the child welfare system are therefore unpaid women (Smith and Smith 1990).

NOTE

1. On March 31, 1991, 54 percent of children in the care of the Minister of Health and Community Services in New Brunswick lived in foster care, 17 percent lived with relatives, 11 percent in group homes, 10 percent with parents, 6 percent in special care institutions and 2 percent out of province (*Child Welfare in Canada* 1994:35).

Chapter 6

Is a Foster Family a Regular Family?

Foster families, just like most other families, suffer from stress and tension and the addition of a foster child to the foster family can create even more. Foster mothers view their care as family care and they try to impart the same values to the foster children as they do to their own children. Foster mothers see their work and role mainly as an extension of their mothering role. They do not view themselves as therapists, social workers or teachers, but as mothers. They provide the child with a safe place, they cook, clean and do the laundry, they drive the child places, they meet with the child's teachers, they meet with social workers, they take the child for visits to the biological parents (albeit in most cases reluctantly), they comfort the child when he or she is hurt or ill, and they discipline when necessary. One of the major differences in a foster family compared to a non-foster family is the temporary nature of fostering. Even though some familial arrangements such as marriages are sometimes temporary in nature, a foster family is often in a constant cycle of transformation that makes foster families a unique living arrangement. In fact many foster families are families in perpetual change.

When a family has just welcomed a foster child the family has to adjust to the new child and the changing intra-familial relationships that result. These changes depend strongly on the needs, behaviour patterns and the length of stay of the foster child. A foster child that has a problem with stealing may not only force physical changes (e.g., locks on doors) in the family home, but may also create discomfort among the foster family members. A foster child who needs much attention may create jealousy in the foster mother's biological children. After the foster family has learned to adapt to the needs of the foster child and the foster child has settled and adjusted to the foster family, s/he must eventually leave. When the foster child leaves, the foster family has to accommodate a return to the familial interactions in place before the foster child arrived.

Foster families renegotiate many of the normally taken-for-granted aspects of family life and this process bears similarities to the struggles of "blended" or reconstituted families (Pasley and Ihinger-Tallman 1987; Neumann-Clubb 1990; Walters 1993). A "blended" family refers to new family arrangements after a separation or divorce when one or both partners engage in new relationships which may include step-parents and step-siblings, etc. A foster family does not entirely fit the characteristics of a "blended" family, for the parents in a foster family are the stable entities and the foster family is created around the child, as opposed to the "blended" family which is created around adults. Further, the "blended" family members, including children, may have a long period in which they can get to know each other. Typically foster families and foster children have no time to get to know each other as the foster child is "brought" into the family by a social worker with little notice to either. When Neumann-Clubb entered a newly reconstituted family by marriage, she experienced "yo-yo feelings" and wondered if it was possible to feel very close to her step-children. She states that "my tolerance level was higher and better for my natural children [than for her step-children]" (1990:61). This particular dilemma was also discussed by some foster mothers. Although all foster mothers interviewed stated that they treated foster children the same as their own, they also had constant doubts about how to be impartial to both their natural and foster children. According to Walters, children in a "blended" family can experience "false expectations, fantasies, divided loyalties, attachment, loss, anger, resentment, fear, and loss of self-esteem" (1993:89). Some of these emotions are also described by the foster mothers concerning their own expectations as well as those some foster children may have. One of the most important expectations of foster mothers is the belief that with the right amount of "love, care and patience" this foster child will "turn around." However, many foster mothers realize, after some time, that many foster children are too traumatized and need more than the "love, care and patience" that they can provide.

Walters argues that if children have not grieved or been able to take time to let go emotionally of the previous family structure, they are unable to form new relationships that will be satisfactory" (1993:91). In most cases, foster children, who are often moved back and forth between their biological and foster families, have little time to grieve for the loss of living with their biological families. When a child is permanently removed from his/her biological family a grieving process can begin but this is not the usual situation.

Again, as in "blended families," some foster children struggled with "divided loyalties" between the foster family and their biological family. In some cases the foster mother experiences divided loyalties between the foster children and her own children. "Blended" family members, in general, have a substantial period of time to work through difficult adjustments; however, this is not the case for foster families. Although some foster placements are longterm, others are very temporary in nature. For example, a foster child may stay for six months, the foster family may be "foster child free" for four months, and then a new foster child may arrive, activating the process of adjustment all over again.

Approximately half of the foster mothers are full-time stay-at-home mothers, the other half work full- or part-time outside the home. Therefore, one of the major similarities between foster families and non-foster families is the balancing act between the demands and needs of the children and the demands of paid labour.

Greta Hofmann Nemiroff argued that married, stay-at-home mothers have three jobs "motherwork, housework and wife/partner work" (1994:195). In addition women who work outside the home have a fourth responsibility: paid work (195). For foster mothers who work outside the home, fostering can be considered a fifth "job." The fostering job is, like all mothering work, mostly carried out in isolation and in the privacy of her home (Rosenberg 1995).

Foster mothers who work outside the home then have to

juxtapose at least five major responsibilities: work, motherwork, housework, wife/partner work and foster-care work. The term "double day" which is used to describe the double responsibilities of working women, seems an understatement for some foster mothers. Many working-for-pay foster mothers probably experience what can be termed the responsibilities of a "triple day."

In this demanding environment, foster mothers make a big effort to treat their foster children like their own. They see their actions towards foster children as rooted in mothering and not in professional caring. They try to make the children feel at home, they comfort them and they often feel saddened when they leave. Nevertheless, fostering has a major impact on the intra-familial relationships. The foster family's own children sometimes have to change their living routines. If the foster mother is married, the couple loses privacy. Despite all these interferences in the foster family members' relationships, the most important impact of fostering is the perpetual change the foster family has to cope with. Foster children come and go, and every time a new foster child comes, new routines have to be established. All the taken-for-granted rules of conduct in a family have to be reiterated when a foster child comes and lives with the family. Fostering has a tremendous impact on the families and lives of women who mother for the state.

This book has provided the reader with a glimpse of the day-to-day lives of foster mothers in Canada. Foster mothers are women who deal with the same issues all mothers deal with except that their motherwork, housework, paid work and wife/partner work is intensified by the demands of the foster child and the demands of the state.

Mothering is a physically and psychologically demanding activity. The feelings of a mother can, in a single day, range from being deeply in love with her children and feeling content to being extremely frustrated by their demands. The question I have been asking myself throughout this study is: Why do women foster? Why do they take on extra responsibilities in addition to the care of their own children? I am not sure if I have a conclusive answer to this question. However, I do feel that women foster for the same reason women choose to be mothers. Hofmann Nemiroff suggests that women mother because:

> Our children reflect back to us visions of ourselves and our reality unhampered by our "official stories" and rationalizations. The relationships enjoyed as mothers are unique in a life often holding other sources for love, affection, and fulfillment: lovers and partners, relatives and colleagues, friends and especially women friends, causes, vocations, work. (1994:199)

Perhaps mothering is the foundation of all human relationships and that is the reason why women still choose to mother. The most intimate relationships mothers have is with their children.

The final paradox is that mothering is a word "that brings forth flamboyant, extravagant, romantic images" (Rosenberg 1995:318), and much lip service is paid to the importance of mothering. Nevertheless, mothering remains an unpaid, isolating experience that is not valued highly in society. As Marilyn Waring so aptly stated in the video *Sex, Lies and the Global Economy,* mothering in a capitalistic, market economy does not contribute to the Gross National Product and therefore is not valued and in fact does not exist. However, on a personal level, mothering can be a very empowering experience. Barbara Shapiro argues that though mothering has restricted her physical freedom, paradoxically, it has brought mental and psychological freedom. Motherhood brought her freedom from "petty career or work anxieties that formerly were capable of obsessing" her, and it increased her self-esteem "through loving and being loved" (1994:185). To sum up simply, foster mothers foster because it makes them feel good about themselves.

Appendix

The information presented in this appendix has been left out of the main text because it is specific to New Brunswick and very detailed. The data presented is entirely based on the survey. More than 600 surveys were sent out to all foster families across New Brunswick, and 275 surveys were returned, a 45 percent return rate. This data provides the reader with a "snapshot" of foster-care services in New Brunswick in 1994.

A PORTRAIT OF FOSTERING IN NEW BRUNSWICK

Of the respondents to the survey, less than one-third of the foster mothers were not actively fostering at the time of the survey. The reasons for this were rather mundane: in 40 percent of the cases the Department of Health and Community Services did not "offer" them foster children. This is partially due to the "lack of children" as well as to the fact that some foster mothers specify what "type" of child they would like to care for; the specifications were mostly age and sometimes gender related. If the Department of Health and Community Services does not have a foster child that fits these specifications, then the foster family may have to wait before a child is placed with them. Table 1 illustrates the reasons why some foster mothers did not have foster children at the time of the survey.

At the time of the survey, the profile of the foster children in care of the foster mothers who responded was as follows: in 61 percent of the cases foster mothers cared for one foster child at a time and in one quarter of the cases the foster mothers cared for two foster children. The rest, 14 percent, of the foster mothers cared for three or more foster children at the time of the survey.

The average length of stay for a foster child in the foster family was almost 2.4 years, and the majority of these foster

Table 1: Reasons for not Actively Fostering

Reasons	%	N
No Children Available	41	33
Need a Break	16	13
Foster Child Left	6	5
System Problems	6	5
Foster Mother had Baby or Job	5	4
Adopted the Foster Child	2	2
Retired	2	2
No Reasons Given	21	17
Total	99	81

children were older children or teenagers with a mean age of 11.6 years. Table 2 illustrates how long foster children have been with the foster family and Table 3 describes the ages of the foster children in care of the foster mothers.

Table 2: Foster Mothers by Time Current Foster Children in Family

Months/Years	%	N
< 3 months	24	42
3–6 months	12	22
6–9 months	6	12
9–12 months	11	19
1–2 years	15	27
2–3 years	9	16
3–4 years	6	10
4–5 years	2	3
5–10 years	14	24
10–16 years	2	4
Total	101	179

Mean: 27.1 months (2.3 years), Mode: 3.0 months, Median: 12.0 months (1 year).

Appendix

Table 3: Age of Foster Children

Age	%	N
< 3 years	16	29
3–6 years	7	12
7–12 years	27	49
13–16 years	32	59
>17 years	18	33
Total	100	182

Mean: 140 months (11.6 years), Mode: 180 months (15 years), Median: 165 months (13.7 years).

Many foster mothers had been fostering for a substantial period of time with an average of 7.1 years and, again, on average, have cared for thirteen foster children during their individual fostering careers (see Table 4).

Table 4: Number of Years Fostered

Years	%	N
1	15	41
2	10	27
3	10	27
4	10	27
5	7	18
6	5	14
7	4	12
8	6	17
9	5	15
10	6	16
11–16	12	32
17–20	3	9
21–30	5	13
31+	1	2
Total	99	270

Mean 7 years; Mode 1 year; Median 5 years.

Table 5. Number of Children Fostered by Foster Families

Children	%	N
1	11	29
2	9	24
3	8	21
4	8	20
5	6	16
6	6	17
7	6	17
8	5	13
9	3	7
10	6	17
11–15	12	31
16–20	6	16
21–30	6	14
31–40	1	4
41–50	1	4
51–100	3	7
100+	3	7
Total	100	264

Mean 13 children; Mode 1 child; Median 7 children.

These last figures (Tables 4 and 5), the average number of years fostered and the average number of children cared for indicate that foster mothers, once they get involved with fostering do not abandon it easily.

CHARACTERIZATION OF FOSTER MOTHERS IN NEW BRUNSWICK

Based on the survey results, foster families live all across New Brunswick and the number of French and English speaking foster parents parallels the linguistic make-up of the province. The first language of the foster mothers was French for roughly one-third of the mothers and English for the other two-thirds. Of the foster parents who answered the survey, 255 (93 percent) were female, 10 (four percent) were male and in 9 (three percent) cases both foster parents responded to the survey. The unstated assumption is that foster parents should preferably be married couples (see Table 6).

Table 6: Marital Status of Foster Mothers

Marital Status	%	N
Married	87	238
Single	3	7
Widowed	2	5
Divorced or Separated	6	17
Common Law Relationship	2	6
Total	100	273

The ages of the foster mothers ranged from 25 to 75 years of age with the majority in their mid-forties and an average age of 42.1 years (see Table 7).

Table 7: Age of Foster Mothers

Age	%	N
25-30 years	7	19
31-35 years	15	40
36-40 years	25	68
41-45 years	21	55
46-50 years	17	47
51-55 years	8	22
56-60 years	3	8
61-65 years	3	7
66 and over	1	3
Total	100	269

Mean: 42 years; Mode: 38 years; Median: 41 years.

Not all foster mothers had children of their own, although most do. Twelve percent (12 percent) had no children or failed to answer the question. The rest of the foster mothers had a number of children ranging from 1 to 25[1] (see Table 8).

Table 8: Number of Own Children (adopted or biological) of Foster Mothers

Number	%	N
1	16	40
2	38	92
3	22	54
4	9	22
5	5	12
6	5	12
7	2	4
8	2	4
21	0	1
25	0	1
Total	99	242

Mean: 3 children; Mode: 2 children; Median: 2 children.

The ages of the oldest "own" child ranged from 1 to 48 years, with an average of 19.2 years and a mode and median of 18 years (see Table 9).

Many foster mothers (80 percent) still had "own" children living at home. Foster mothers and their families lived predominantly in rural areas (81 percent). The vast majority (89 percent) of foster mothers reported involvement in religion. The majority adhered to Roman Catholicism (see Table 10). The rest were divided among various denominations such as: Baptists, United Church, Anglicans, Pentecostals, Presbyterians, Wesleyans, Methodists and the Church of Christ.

Table 9: Age of Oldest Own (adopted or biological) Child of Foster Mothers

Years	%	N
1-5	7	15
6-10	14	33
11-15	17	39
16-20	18	40
21-25	16	36
26-30	16	37
31-35	7	16
36-40	3	7
41 and over	2	5
Total	100	228

Mean: 19 years; Mode: 18 years; Median: 18 years.

Table 10: Religious Affiliation of Foster Mothers

Religion	%	N
Roman Catholic	61	117
Baptist	13	26
United Church	9	17
Anglican	6	11
Pentecostal	6	11
Wesleyan	3	5
Other	3	5
Total	101	192

Of the foster mothers, 55 percent did not work outside the home, 25.7 percent work full-time and 20 percent work part-time outside the home. The occupations they practised were wide ranging from hairdresser or short-order cook to manager or nurse. On an educational level, almost half of the foster mothers had finished high school (48 percent). Thirteen percent had a couple of years of college or had a community college degree, nine percent had a university degree and the rest (almost 30 percent) had an education of grade 11 or less (see Table 11).

Table 11: Education of Foster Mothers

Education	%	N
Grade 10 or less	29	67
Grade 12	48	108
Community College	9	20
Some University	5	11
Bachelor's Degree	7	16
Postgraduate Degree	2	5
Total	100	227

Of the spouses, 64 percent worked full-time and 17 percent worked part-time outside the home, and 19 percent did not work outside the home. The professions of the spouses also covered a wide range of occupations from labourer to university professor. The educational level of the spouses was, on average, lower than that of foster mothers with only 36.1 percent having finished high school (see Table 12).

Table 12: Education of Foster Mothers' Spouses

Education	%	N
Grade 8 or less	19	32
Grades 9 - 10	23	38
Grades 11-12	36	61
Community College	7	12
Bachelor's Degree	11	19
Postgraduate Degree	4	7
Total	100	169

All the occupations of the foster mothers and their spouses were coded according to an index for occupations, the Blishen Scale (Blishen and McRoberts 1976). This index of occupations must be seen as a loose guide because much of the data provided in this category by the survey respondents was incomplete or not very specific. The Blishen Scale ranges from 1 to 500, 1 being the highest socio-economic occupation and 500 the lowest. The mean level of occupation of the foster mothers reached a score of 272, considerably higher than that of their spouses who reached a mean score of 323 (Tables 13 and 14).

Table 13: Category of Occupation of Foster Mothers

Level*	%	N
Group 1 (1-100)	15	24
Group 2 (101-200)	14	23
Group 3 (201-300)	26	42
Group 4 (301-400)	22	35
Group 5 (401-500)	23	36
Total	100	160

*1 highest level; 500 lowest level) Mean: 272; Mode: 297; Median: 297.

Table 14: Category of Occupation of Foster Mothers' Spouses

Level*	%	N
Group 1 (1-100)	8	16
Group 2 (101-200)	11	21
Group 3 (201-300)	13	25
Group 4 (301-400)	30	57
Group 5 (401-500)	38	73
Total	100	192

*1 highest level; 500 lowest level) Mean: 323; Mode: 440; Median: 368.

FOSTER MOTHERS' DAILY ACTIVITIES

Foster mothers reported spending much time on domestic activities with childcare, including helping the child with homework, being the second largest responsibility (Table 15).

Table 15: Daily Fostering Activities Performed by Foster Mothers

Activities	%	N	Mean Times Performed
Domestic Chores	90	248	3.2
Childcare	62	169	2.0
Leisure	26	71	1.6
Spouse	4	10	1.0
Paid Work	20	56	1.0
Help child with homework	44	120	1.0

Because of the increased workload, most foster mothers said that fostering affected their typical day considerably (Table 16).

Table 16: Impact of Fostering on a Typical Day

Level of Impact	%	N
Hardly	24	60
Moderately	35	88
Greatly	41	102
Total	100	250

Answers to the open-ended questions when analyzed revealed three major issues that influenced foster mothers' daily routines. First, fostering created extra work. Secondly, fostering brought with it much interference in day-to-day activities from others.[2] Thirdly, the stress levels in the foster mothers' lives increased as a result of the bigger workload and the different people they had to deal with.

Some of the foster mothers who felt that their day-to-day

activities were "greatly" affected by fostering, described their experiences as follows: "Extra daily workload. Extra time required to deal with social worker, doctors, school, natural parents, extra stress" (1253). Or: "It is an additional responsibility: another person to keep track of, do laundry for and provide a meal for" (1121). Those foster mothers who felt that fostering affected their day-to-day activities "moderately", described their experiences as follows: "Gives me more than I would normally do. Also gives me a boost helping someone—phone calls from previous children to thank you" (1197).

Another mother stated:

> My day starts at 6:30 and ends at twelve midnight. Being a foster parent doesn't change my day much. It depends on the needs of each child in my home. You just cook a bit more and wash a bit more. I try to give each child as much love and attention as I can. The work waits until the children are in bed. (1095)

The foster mothers who felt that their day to day activities were "hardly" or not at all affected by fostering described their days as follows: "It doesn't affect my day hardly at all; you just treat them and do for them like you do your own children. Some children offer a challenge but its still rewarding" (1440). Or: "Being a foster parent really doesn't affect my typical day. You adjust your time for things a little more without realizing it. The things I do most days are things that have to be done anyway; what's a few more minutes of your time?" (1535).

What type of activities were responsible for the increased workload and the higher stress levels in foster mothers' daily routines? Two grids were utilized to collect data measuring the frequency of routine activities foster mothers engaged in and the stress levels associated with their personal relationships. In these two grids, the respondents' answer could range from "often/ weekly" to "never" or "not applicable." Table 17 illustrates that most foster mothers prepared school lunches for the foster child, helped the foster child with school work and drove them regularly to various places. The above mentioned activities can be seen as "normal" childcare activities. However, a number of activities different from non-foster families emerged. Almost sixty percent of foster mothers reported daily talks with the foster child about her/his problems. These "talks" could range from informal chats to formal, almost counselling-like, sessions.

Table 17: Routine Fostering Activities Performed by Foster Mothers

Routine Activities %	Daily	Weekly	Rarely	Never	N/A	Total %
Driving	39	50	3	1	7	100
Talking about problems	59	23	5	1	12	100
Preparing lunch	75	9	4	3	9	100
Discussing house rules	33	39	11	5	12	100
Helping with home work	50	19	6	3	22	100
Family outings	22	47	20	2	9	100
Talking to social worker	13	53	26	1	7	100
Talking to child's friends	23	37	14	8	18	100
Visiting child's friends	12	43	23	5	17	100
Discussing TV watching	18	29	25	11	17	100
Talking to child's teacher(s)	10	32	34	6	18	100
Talking to child's parent(s)	8	34	25	14	19	100
Visiting child's family	9	32	22	16	21	100
Arguing with child	7	29	25	21	18	100
Talking to child's doctor	4	16	53	13	14	100

Other issues that emerged and seemed strongly related to the specific needs of foster families were the frequent discussions around house-rules and television viewing. More than seventy percent of the foster mothers reported that discussing house rules took place at least weekly with the foster child. When the category "argue about chores and house rules" was added, it became a frequently reoccurring activity. When the debates concerning television watching were included in the category "discussion around house rules," it became apparent that foster mothers spend an enormous amount of time discussing rules of conduct around the house with the foster children. All in all, a picture emerged that taking care of a foster child does involve a lot more than physical care. Emotional care, demonstrated by the amount of time foster mothers spend "counselling," "discussing" and "arguing" with the foster children was a very significant part of the day-to-day activities of foster mothers.

The amount of outside contact with others such as social workers was a major issue that created work and stress in the life of foster mothers. More than 50 percent of the foster mothers reported that they talked to a social worker weekly and 13 percent reported talking to a social worker daily. A further significant number of foster mothers talked to the foster child's teacher weekly. One-third of the foster mothers reported that they had weekly contacts with the foster child's parents.

Another important issue that can be abstracted from Table 17 relates to how foster mothers integrate foster children into their own families. Many foster mothers reported that they took the foster children on family outings or when they visited friends. The number of foster mothers who reported that they never took the foster children on family outings or to visit friends was small; in some cases it is possible that the foster children were too old to take on visits or family outings.

In conclusion, the day-to-day activities of foster mothers were very much located in "what mothers do": making lunches, driving children places and helping children with homework. The "counselling" aspect that foster mothers were engaged in and the amount of time spent on dealing with the foster child's conduct at home are activities that go beyond regular or routine mothering activities and may be peculiar to caring for a foster child. Although foster mothers had an increased physical workload, they also had an increased emotional workload dealing with highly sensitive, agitated, temperamental and hurt children who did not always behave in a manner that was satisfactory to the foster mother.

FOSTER MOTHERS AND STRESS

It is clear from Table 17 that being a foster mother increased the number of daily activities and changed the daily routines considerably, resulting in added stress to the personal relationships. Table 18 demonstrates the degree of relationship stress felt by foster mothers. The most significant issue to emerge was the notion that the relationship between the foster mother and the foster child was quite stressful. Almost one quarter of the foster mothers reported a stressful situation occurring weekly between them and the foster child and eight percent reported daily stress. Only one-quarter of the foster mothers reported that they never had a stressful moment with the foster child.

Table 18: Foster Mothers' Stress in Relationships

Stress with (%)	Daily	Weekly	Monthly	Never	N/A	Total
Foster child	8	25	23	26	18	100
Own children	6	23	30	25	16	100
Teacher	6	16	20	44	14	100
Spouse	4	17	31	35	13	100
Social worker	3	13	24	50	10	100
Own parents	3	7	13	59	18	100
Neighbours	1	5	15	67	12	100
Own siblings	2	6	12	64	16	100
Parents-in-law	0	2	8	65	25	100
Church members	0	2	6	68	24	100

Foster mothers reported that stress levels with their own children were not much lower than with their foster children. By contrast, though, the stress levels with spouses were perceived to be lower. This can mean two things: the relationship between mothers and children is often a cause of significant tension in general, or it can mean that when a mother becomes a foster mother the tension with the foster children increases the tension with her own children.

The farther the foster mother was removed from a relationship, the less stress she reported. Nevertheless tension levels with others were still notable. Almost 40 percent of the foster mothers reported that they often, weekly or monthly, had a stressful moment with the foster child's teacher. The incidence of stress in the relationship between the foster mother and the social worker was somewhat lower than with the teacher. Although some of the stressful events reported may have occurred in the foster families regardless of the foster child, it is nevertheless clear that when a woman becomes a foster mother, a significant amount of tension enters into her life.

FOSTER MOTHERS' MOTIVATION

Respondents were asked to describe the rewards of being a foster mother. The results are described in Table 19. Half of the foster mothers reported wanting to continue to foster because fostering "makes them feel good." More than one-third of the foster mothers claimed that the most rewarding aspect of fostering was related to what they could do for the child: "to make a difference in the child's life" or "to provide a safe place for the child." Other rewards included the belief that foster mothers' biological children "learned to share" their resources and their parents' personal relationships.

Table 19: Rewards of Foster Care as Described by Foster Mothers

Rewards	%	N
Factors related to foster parent(s)	50	132
Factors related to foster child	34	89
Factors related to foster family	10	25
Sharing	6	16
Total	100	262

Some foster mothers described the rewards of fostering as wanting to see the foster children change. The desired changes were characterized as follows: "it makes me feel good to see a child that has been with us for three years go to university to become a real professional and be proud of what they are doing" (1551). Or: "Watching a child grow and be more able to control themselves and become responsible for themselves" (1081).

Again another foster mother stated:

> The most positive or rewarding aspect for me is knowing that being there as a foster parent could make some kind of difference in a child's life. When you get your first hug, when you know the child you're caring for has positive responses, just knowing you offer all your love and protection to a child in times of difficulty. (1440)

Or:

> Helping a victim of sexual abuse develop into a survivor
> of sexual abuse. Seeing them regaining self worth, self
> esteem and confidence and no longer think they deserved
> or asked for it. I help with their pain and in turn it works
> as therapy for me and makes me even more determined to
> get involved and make a little difference in their lives.
> Their achievements are rewarding to me. (1047)

Thus the rewards of fostering were non-material in nature, but
obviously convincing enough for the foster mothers to stay involved with fostering despite the increased tension levels, increased workload and increased interference in their daily routines.

WHAT WERE THE CHALLENGES FOR FOSTER MOTHERS?

In some ways, the most difficult or challenging aspect of fostering
was an extension of what foster mothers saw as their rewards.
Table 20 shows what most foster mothers considered the most
difficult aspect of fostering. The greatest challenge in foster care
was also the greatest reward: to make a child respond to the
foster mothers' efforts and affection. Most foster children were so
hurt by the time they arrived in a foster home that they were hard
to "reach" and many displayed difficult and/or deviant behaviour. As a result of the abuse, the children did not trust adults and
often the children could not be trusted. This type of behaviour,
the lack of trust, was reported by foster mothers as being a very
difficult and frustrating challenge to cope with.

A second issue that was frustrating for many foster mothers
was their concern for the child who was sent back to the natural
parents when the foster mothers felt that nothing had changed in
that environment. In these cases foster mothers felt that all their
work and efforts were in vain.

Other challenges reported by foster mothers were related to a
variety of issues ranging from the relationships between the
foster mother and the child's parents, and the difficulties the
"system" created. However, more than 105 foster mothers reported that the most challenging and difficult aspect of fostering

Table 20: Challenges in Foster Care as Described by Foster Mothers

Challenges	%	N
Traumatized kids, lack of trust, knowing child's needs	46	121
Returning child to unchanged home	14	35
Sharing, fairness	13	34
No support services, social worker	9	24
Biological parents	8	19
Maintaining emotional distance from child	10	27
Total	100	260

was that they got too attached to the children. As a result when the children left, the foster mothers were left grieving.

Analyzing the data surrounding this question revealed a pattern of difficulties that were circular in nature. The initial challenges in foster care were also the ultimate rewards: transforming the child into a happy person. Further, foster mothers reported that the initial behaviour of many foster children posed many challenges and disruptions to the family. In addition, foster mothers had to cope with intrusions in their day-to-day activities from the child's parent(s), the "system" and others.

Some foster mothers expressed their feelings concerning the challenges in foster care as follows:

> The most difficult thing to see is when the child is returned to the same environment. This is called the yo-yo. He leaves, then returns. I have had children who have been returned to their parents eight to ten times in a two-year period. It is not fair for the child. Often the return of the child occurs after the parents have gotten their seasonal cheques or the income tax credits for the child. (1438)

Another mother listed the difficulties she had experienced:

1. Department cutbacks. 2 No programs for teenagers. 3. Children being forced to go back home. 4. Natural family can be harmful in some cases. 5. Foster parents' views are often overlooked. 6. Feelings of being kept in the dark. (1079)

A third mother also struggled with her feelings after the children left:

Letting go and wondering are they okay, have they eaten, and carrying on with your life. It is also difficult because others do not realize the love and bond between you, your family and the child. When my now fifteen-year-old was born, I had a placement that had been with us a while and was going for adoption, and I remember thinking I'd rather see my baby go, who I wanted so dearly. I felt very bad about that at the time. (1167)

Another foster mother described the challenge:

The challenge is to help the child become a happy fully functioning human being. The difficulty is hanging onto some scraps of my own life. Disapproval of my methods by siblings, foster parents, neighbours, teachers etc. are very draining. Could use a lot more support from social worker. (1164)

This foster mother described what sometimes happened after the children left:

I guess the challenging aspect is when they come back to visit and they seem so happy to see us. Like the two boys we had for a couple of months, when they came to visit for a week, about three months after they left, they didn't want to leave us again. The baby hung right on around my neck. That's when it is difficult, when you have to force their little arms from around your neck and pass them over. (1217)

The difficulties and the challenges the foster mothers experienced were complex but often could be traced back to the "system." They were willing to deal with difficult children but they found it arduous to let go, particularly when they believed that the child was returned to an "unchanged" home environment, thereby defeating all the energy, love and dedication the foster mother had invested in the foster child.

THEIR RELATIONSHIP WITH FOSTER CHILDREN

Even though foster mothers reported that their relationship with their foster children displayed the highest tension levels of all their close relationships, the majority of the foster mothers reported a positive relationship with their foster children (81 percent). Ten percent of the foster mothers stated that they felt that the child was indifferent to them, the rest, another 10 percent, felt that the foster children were neither negative nor positive.

As is the nature of foster care, at some point in time the foster child will leave the foster family. The reasons are documented in Table 21.

Table 21: Reasons why Foster Children Leave Foster Families

Reason	%	N
Returned home	56	111
Problems with foster child	11	22
Adopted	11	22
On their own	8	16
Other foster home	6	12
Run away	3	6
Other	5	13
Total	100	202

No matter why the child left foster care, most foster mothers reported being upset at the time of the departure (78 percent). The rest, 22 percent, felt good or relieved that the foster child had left. These results are consistent with reports that for many foster mothers the major challenge was to "let go."

This "letting go" was made more difficult by feelings of worry or anger on the part of the foster mother. For example, foster mothers worried for the child's future. One foster mother reported being upset because: "arrangements were done without my knowledge" (1051). Another foster mother reported: "Failure, disappointed" (1309). A foster mother who had grown very attached to the foster child she had cared for stated that she felt: "Sad. They were three and five years old and we had them for one and half years. You get quite attached" (1231). Again another mother felt that she had failed the foster child; she recalled:

> I felt I had failed. I felt the Department had failed. The social worker only saw him once every six months. I had requested they get him help and they wouldn't. I feel there is nothing else I could've done for him. (1206)

Or: "Disappointed because she returned to the same environment" (1230). One foster mother stated that she felt "terrible, I missed them so much, I cried" (1201). Or as another foster mother reported: "sad, we wonder if we did enough or what we could have done so that the child would have stayed" (1507).

Other foster mothers felt more satisfied with the outcome of the separation. One reported that she felt "empty but glad as it was a successful adoption placement. When you have siblings longterm and they leave all at once it is sort of like being laid off from a longterm job because your whole life and purpose changes" (1058). Another stated: "My heart was broken, not my spirit, and I knew I gave him my all for the year he was with us. Happy too!" (1167). Yet another foster mother stated "she was only fifteen months when she left. She came when she was six months. This was really hard on all of us family "(1097). Few foster mothers expressed feelings of relief such as this foster mother who felt "relieved and hopeful for his future" (1293) when the foster child left her care.

Many foster mothers had mixed feelings oscillating between relief and being upset concerning the foster child's departure. One foster mother stated: "I had mixed feelings about my last child, because I didn't feel she was ready, she was a mixed up little girl" (1217). Or: "Happy and relief. But also disappointed of not having been able to make a change or help" (1227). Or: "Very upset in regards to her future. But reassured by the fact that she was loved and happy with her time with us" (1200). Many foster mothers reported being very worried about the foster child when the child returned to the home environment that the foster mothers felt had not changed.

A second issue that emerged was that foster mothers very much appreciated it when they were able to stay "in touch" with the foster child after s/he had left their care. The foster mothers had invested so much emotional energy in the foster child that they found it difficult to suddenly be cut off from him or her.

The last issue that emerged from this portion of the analysis was that foster mothers would like to be consulted about the foster child's future. Often foster mothers felt that the child was absolutely not ready for [yet] another move. However, because of court decisions or a decision made by the social worker(s), the child had to be moved, increasing the anxiety concerning the child's future on the part of the foster mother.

THEIR RELATIONSHIP WITH THE DEPARTMENT OF HEALTH AND COMMUNITY SERVICES

Just under eight in every ten foster mothers answered that their relationship with the Department of Health and Community Services was "mostly positive" (79 percent=210). While around 10 percent (n=25) of the foster mothers reported that their experiences were "sometimes positive" and "sometimes negative," a further 7 percent (n=17) reported that their experience was "neither positive nor negative" and 5 percent (n=14) reported that their experience was "negative."

One foster mother saw her relationship with the Department of Health and Community Services as a positive one, although she did acknowledge that it could be improved. She stated: "We can openly express our feelings to the Department and even though our opinions don't carry a lot of weight they are acknowledged and noted and some day may have a part in a child's life" (1253). Another foster mother stated: "They are mainly positive, but [we] had ones that are very bad" (1081). Again another foster mother described her relationship with the Department of Health and Community Services as: "I must say most of my workers have been super!" (1226). Or: "Positive. They always are attentive to the family and the children placed in foster care. There is good supervision" (1473).

However, not everybody was pleased with their relationship with the Department of Health and Community Services. The following story is from a foster mother who felt very poorly treated by the Department, although, at the same time she also praised a social worker for helping her through this difficult period.

> Our family was nearly destroyed by a social worker. We had a two-year-old male child and a twelve-year-old male was placed there for thirty days. This child had a history of sexual abuse and when I discovered that he may have been a perpetrator, I asked to have him removed (after fourteen days). The worker was very angry and wrote a report for our file stating that I was unbalanced and dangerous. We were not informed about this until two years later when we tried to have our adoption status updated. The adoption worker refused to approve our home because he had proof that I was "unstable and a danger to any child placed in my home." It took us over a year to get this mess cleared up and caused a lot of problems for our family and our extended families. If we had not been so determined to see this through and had we not had a very supportive child protection worker for the child in our home, everyone's life would be very different. No, I cannot recommend fostering to anyone because I am still very bitter. We should not have to fight so hard to do the job we do. (1146)

Another foster mother also felt mistreated by the Department of Health and Community Services; she stated:

> It was always positive until we moved to a large home. They came to evaluate us and made us feel very uneasy, as if they did not feel we were capable of doing the job. They wanted to verify all sorts of things (it was compli-

cated). One time when the children were out, they accused me of not spending the money sent to me on the children's clothing because they did not have enough. This was not true and I was very disappointed. Before we moved the social workers told us that we were the best foster family. (1638)

Although the relationship between the foster mother and the social worker may have been occasionally "rocky," when there was a problem, foster mothers turned to the social worker for help (see Table 22).

Table 22: Person(s) Foster Mothers Turn to for Support

Person	%	N
Social worker	63	164
Spouse	21	55
Other foster parent(s)	7	17
Friends	5	13
Family	4	10
Total	100	259

Although the relationship between the foster mothers and the social workers seems to be by and large a positive one, that did not mean that the foster mothers did not want improvements. Most of the changes foster mothers would like to see were related to the "system" (see Table 23). Some of the foster mothers who answered that aspects of the "system" should change, suggested the following: "more communication with social worker" (1051); "more training—more access to follow-up on children returned "(1058).

Another foster mother stated: "A better understanding and cooperation with our social workers. Not to make you feel like this is your duty to take these children or when they make you feel unworthy or that you've done something wrong. Or have some that think they know all and your feelings don't count" (1535).

Or: "More social workers with small case loads. Less change in staff" (1135). Again another foster mother stated:

Table 23: Changes Foster Mothers Would Like in Foster Care

Suggestions	%	N
Related to system (more money, improve image, better evaluation)	45	92
Related to foster family (take foster parents seriously, balance rights of foster and biological parents)	21	43
Continuity of care (follow child, more social workers, more communication)	12	26
Related to biological parents (more accountability, earlier removal of child)	5	11
Some changes	4	8
No complaints	14	29
Total	101	209

As with many government programs underfunded, for example, when a child needs eye-glasses, they are allowed to pick from a pre-selected array of frames—almost always noticeable as welfare glasses—I will pay the difference to ensure they are the same as "other kids" wear! When you consider daycare costs [of] nine [to] eleven dollars [for an] eight to five [pm] day per child and [compare it to] the amount [of] involvement in foster care, one must consider it a job of love—for certain. (1331)

Or: "I would like to see foster parents get paid an hourly wage, so at least it would be a little more financially rewarding when you sit frozen in a hockey rink for eight or ten hours" (1267).

Many foster mothers felt that they should be taken more seriously by the Department of Health and Community Services. One foster mother expressed it as follows: "I would like to see the foster parents being more of a decision maker on behalf of the child instead of the social worker and the Department being totally in control" (1253). Or: "The image of foster parents seems to be so bad. If this was addressed we could attract better families or at least more families to deal with the need" (1174). Or: "I would like to see more cooperation between the foster home, natural family and social worker" (1226).

Continuity of care for the children was something foster mothers would like to see implemented. As one foster mother stated: "I believe whatever worker is originally assigned to the child, that worker should continue to be the child's worker until the child leaves care" (1171). Or: "More real case planning and solid commitment to follow the plan. A better balance between the child's rights and the natural parents' rights. Something in place so the child does not have to change workers when he becomes a permanent ward. More commitment from the Department toward older children" (1081).

Some foster parents felt that the parents of the foster child needed to carry more responsibility. "Try to find some way (I don't know how) to assess the natural family earlier so that if a child is not going to be returned they don't have to be bounced back and forth many times" (1218). Or: "Regular check up with foster parents; a closer survey of natural parents before a child returns home" (1526). Or: "The foster parent having a greater role in setting the plan and implementing it. To see a joint effort between foster parents, natural parents and workers that puts the child first. That everyone works together on a mutually agreed upon plan. Workers have too much power over the child, the parents and the foster parents" (1096). Or: "I would like the system of the minister to protect the rights of the child and less of the parents. I have seen children returned to be with abusive natural parents crying, throwing themselves on the ground, refusing to go but forced anyway" (1438).

The overall relationship between the foster mothers and the social worker was a positive one based on the fact that in times of crisis his or her help was sought, although in reality foster mothers do not have anywhere else to turn except the social worker. Foster mothers were not free to discuss the foster child's problems with friends because of confidentiality policies concerning the foster child. Thus in practice foster mothers can only seek help from the social worker when they want to discuss issues concerning their foster child.

REASONS FOR BECOMING A FOSTER MOTHER

The fourth part of the survey consisted of eight questions related to the foster mothers or foster families' decisions to become and remain a foster family. Responses to "Why did you become a foster family?" generated a wide range of responses. The majority of women who became foster mothers wanted to help a child, to love them, to care for them and to provide a safe environment for them to grow up (52 percent). For example, one foster mother stated that she wanted to help: "because there is a great need for these children. When we can help a child it warms our hearts" (1340). Another mother stated: "We wanted to enlarge our family, we have two girls (twins). The risks of another pregnancy, the loss of our first child due to spina bifida. Big house. The desire to help our young" (1342). Foster mothers who wanted to provide a family for foster children wanted: "[t]o help children who are neglected and to give them a good time in a family" (1557). Another mother stated: "To help or try to help many out there. Give them the opportunity to live in a family situation when they can be cared for where everyone is invited to make mistakes and talk about them" (1552).

Women, who became foster mothers because fostering was in one way or another a part of their upbringing or a part of a family member's background, mentioned that they wanted to "repay a debt." One foster mother stated: "To repay the debts of someone else being foster parents to my father and husband. To share our parenting skills to someone in need" (1253). Or: "Originally we started because my husband had spent time in a N.B. orphanage and he wanted to repay the debt. Our plan was to foster for a year" (1081).

Foster mothers who were categorized as having "other" reasons for getting involved in fostering responded as follows: "My family is grown up and gone and the house after years of having children of my own seemed very empty and quiet. Some of my co-workers are foster parents and told me we could liven up my home and also help someone in need of a good home" (1248). Or, as one foster mother stated: "Ultimately, to provide a service to the community" (1198).

The fact that, for many women, the reasons for becoming a foster mother were related to wanting to help children may explain why many foster mothers reported that they initiated the first contact with the Department of Health and Community Services (48 percent).

Table 24: How Families became Foster Families

Contact	%	N
HCS	48	126
Friends	18	47
Advertisement	14	38
Family	8	20
Knew child	4	10
Social worker	3	7
Clergy	1	4
Other	4	12
Total	100	264

A further 18 percent reported having become involved with foster care through friends. More than 13 percent of the foster mothers reported having responded to an advertisement. The rest were divided between knowing a child that was in need of care, and a clergy member or a social worker encouraging them to get involved. It seemed that informal channels for recruiting new foster mothers were more successful than formal ones.

In order to assess, from a different angle, how foster mothers felt about foster care, the respondents were asked what advice they would give to would-be foster families. The responses, which were diverse, were collapsed into five major categories.

Based on the impact fostering has on the daily routines of these foster mothers, it is obvious why the item "time, love and patience" is so important. It is the type of advice which is easy to understand and supports the earlier statement made by foster mothers about the increased workload when one starts to foster. For example, one foster mother stated that "one needs a lot of patience, understanding, and to be able to put yourself in the child's place" (1593). Another mother stated: "do it, give the most of yourself and love the child as you would your own" (1557). A third foster mother's advice was as follows: "be sure you have a

Table 25: Advice Foster Mothers Would Give to Others

Advice related to	%	N
Time, love and patience	32	81
Foster families (positive)	22	57
Foster families (negative)	20	50
Foster child	12	31
System	14	35
Total	100	254

lot of extra time and an abundance of patience because this process requires one hundred percent of both" (1248).

Many foster mothers wanted to advise prospective foster families that they should not expect a "Walton Family" child. One mother stated: "try not to expect too much from the child, do not expect gratitude and try to treat them like your own" (1171). Another foster mother warned that prospective foster parents should not have very high expectations of fostering. She argued that one should be "prepared for disappointment by both the child and Department" (1079). Or as another foster mother stated, the experience can be mixed. "Be prepared for both good and hard times. Try to be very understanding everyday. Be ready to extend your family for the child that comes to your home and needs to feel wanted and cared for" (1136). Or: "Not to have any unrealistic expectations about the foster kids or Community Services regarding support for them "(1161).

Almost one-quarter of the foster mothers would advise prospective foster families that fostering can have a positive influence on their own family. For example, one foster mother stated: "If you have the love for a foster child and room, it is rewarding to take them in your home and give the love and attention they need" (1286).

Another group of foster mothers felt that negative comments concerning fostering should be ignored. One foster mother replied: "Don't listen to the negative feedback from family and 'friends.' Listen to your own hearts and go for it but realize that these children aren't all from the 'Walton Family'" (1058). Although much advice was positive in nature, at least 20 percent of the foster mothers' advice was not positive. For example, one foster mother's advice was to get informed about the system. She stated: "Assure yourself by going to get as many instructions as possible to give yourself a better feeling about the system and the work that is involved" (1571). Another foster mother advised prospective foster parents to remember the hierarchy: "Always keep in mind that they are not yours. The Department is the guardian and can and will move the child whenever they want, and how you feel about decisions always comes third. Child, Department, you" (1081). Another foster mother advised prospective foster parents against fostering when they had their own children at home. She stated: "don't if you have any children in your home" (1146). Some Foster mothers felt that parents should get involved with fostering for the "right reasons" because it was a very demanding responsibility. "Examine your motives, make a list of what you and your family might have to sacrifice and what things you will find rewarding. Make sure everyone is okay with it. Be prepared to be patient" (1179).

Many foster mothers are extremely committed to foster care and the advice foster mothers would give to other prospective foster families supports that commitment. Although some advice was negative in nature, with a few foster mothers saying: "Do not do it!" the majority felt that fostering was an enriching experience for the entire family.

Foster Mothers' Recommendations for Fostering

An indicator of how foster mothers viewed fostering is provided by their answers to the question: "Would you recommend to other families to become a foster family?" Three-quarters (n=202) of the foster mothers responded with a "yes," almost one-quarter with a "qualified yes"—depends on the family and child (n=60)— and only 3 percent with a solid "no." A further indication of the commitment to foster care by foster mothers was the fact that more than two-thirds (n=169) of the foster mothers would take another foster child when their current foster child has left. Another one in five (n=54) foster mothers responded that they would take another foster child in their home depending on family circumstances and the characteristics of the foster child, while only 7 percent (n=17) asserted that they would not take a foster child when their current foster child left.

NOTES

1. Two foster mothers had twenty-one and twenty-five children; many of these children were adopted. I did not make a distinction between adopted and biological children. Under the *Family Services Act* (1980) adoptive and biological parents have the same responsibilities.
2. The term "others" can mean anybody who is not part of the immediate family but has contact with the foster child, such as a social worker, school teacher, therapist, etc.

References

Aries, Phillippe. 1962. *Centuries of Childhood*. New York: Random House.

Badinter, Elisabeth. 1981. *Mother Love*. New York: MacMillan.

Baker, Patricia.1996. *Hearing and Writing Women's Voices*. Paper presented at the conference Praxis/Nexus: Feminist Methodology, Theory, Community, Victoria, B.C. Jan. 19–20.

Barrett, Michele, and Mary McIntosh. 1991. *The Anti-social Family*. London: Verso.

Barter, Kenneth A. 1994. "The Foster Care Crisis Management Practices in Public Child Welfare Systems: An Issues of Partnership—Philosophy and Practice in Temporary Foster Care." *Community Alternatives* Vol. 6, 2(Fall).

Berridge, David, and Hedy Cleaver. 1987. *Foster Home Breakdown*. New York: Blackwell.

Blishen, Bernard R., and Hugh McRoberts. 1976. "A Revised Socioeconomic Index for Occupations in Canada." *Canadian Review of Sociology and Anthropology* 15.

Boswell, John. 1988. *Kindness of Strangers*. New York: Vintage.

Canada. 1994. *Child Welfare in Canada*. Ottawa: Federal–Provincial Working Group on Child and Family Services Information.

Carbino, Rosemarie. 1991. "Advocacy for Foster Families in the United States Facing Child Abuse Allegations: How Social Agencies and Foster Parents are Responding to the Problem." *Child Welfare* Vol LXX, 2, (March-April).

Child Welfare in Canada. 1994. Ottawa: Federal–Provincial Working Groups on Child and Family Services Information.

Chodorow, Nancy. 1978. *The Reproduction of Mothering: Psychoanalysis and the Sociology of Gender*. Berkley: University of California Press.

Cohen, Joyce S., and Anne Westhues. 1990. *Well-Functioning Families for Adoptive and Foster Children*. University of Toronto Press.

Currie, Dawn. 1986. "The Transformation of Juvenile Justice in Canada: A Study of Bill C-61." In Brian MacLean (ed.), *Political Economy of Crime*. Scarborough: Prentice Hall.

Descarries-Belanger, Francine, and Shirley Roy. 1991. *The Women's Movement and Its Currents of Thought: A Typological Essay*. Ottawa: CRIAW/ICREF.

Donzelot, Jacques. 1979. *The Policing of Families*. New York: Random House.

Eichler, Margrit. 1983. *Families in Canada Today*. Toronto: Gage.

Eichler, Margrit, and Jeanne Lapointe. 1985. *On the Treatment of the Sexes in Research*. Ottawa: Social Science and Humanities Research Council of Canada.

Family Services Act. 1985. Province of New Brunswick, Fredericton.

Forcey, Linda Rennie. 1987. *Mothers of Sons: Towards an Understanding of Responsibility*. New York: Praeger.

Galaway, Burt, Richard Nutter, and Joe Hudson. 1994. "Birth Parent Participation in Treatment Foster Family Care." In Brad McKenzie (ed.), *Current Perspectives on Foster Family Care for Children and Youth*. Toronto: Wall & Emerson.

Gomme, Ian. 1995. "Education." In Robert Brym (ed.), *New Society: Sociology for the 21st Century*. Toronto: Harcourt Brace.

Goode, William J. 1963. *World Revolution and Family Patterns*. New York: The Free Press.

Gordon, Collin. 1980. *Power/knowledge*. New York: Pantheon.

Hepworth, H. Phillip. 1980. *Foster Care and Adoption in Canada*. Ottawa: Canadian Council on Social Development.

Hiley, Michael. 1979. *Victorian Working Women*. London: Gordon Fraser.

Hochschild, Arlie. 1989. *The Second Shift: Working Parents and the Revolution at Home*. New York: Viking Penguin.

Hofmann Nemiroff, Greta. 1994 "Reflections on Motherhood." In Maureen T. Reddy, Martha Roth and Amy Sheldon (eds.), *Mother Journeys: Feminists Write about Mothering*. Minneapolis: Spinster Ink.

Jones, Deborah. 1998. "Canada's Real Adoption Crisis."

Chatelaine, May 1998:53.

Kaplan, Meryle Mahrer. 1992. *Mother's Images of Motherhood.* London: Routledge.

Kendrick, Martin. 1990. *Nobody's Children.* Toronto: MacMillan.

Kufeldt, Kathleen. 1991. "Foster Care: A Reconceptualization." *Community Alternatives* Vol 3, 1 (Spring):9–17.

———. 1994. "Inclusive Foster Care: Implementation of The Model." In Brad Mckenzie (ed.), *Current Perspectives on Foster Family Care for Children and Youth.* Toronto: Wall & Emerson.

Lemay, Raymond A. 1991. "Against the Professionalization of Foster Care: An Essay." *The Social Worker/Le travailleur social* 59, 3 (Fall/Automme).

Luxton, Meg. 1980. *More Than a Labour of Love.* Toronto: Women's Press.

———. 1995. "Two Hands on the Clock: Changing Patterns in the Gendered Division of Labour in the Home." In E.D. Nelson and B.W. Robinson (eds.), *Gender in the 1990s.* Toronto: Nelson.

Mackie, Marlene. 1984. "Socialization: Changing Views of Child Rearing and Adolescence." In Maureen Baker (ed.), *The Family: Changing Trends in Canada.* Toronto: McGraw-Hill Ryerson.

Maluccio, Anthony N., Robin Warsh, and Barbara A Pine. 1993. "Rethinking Family Reunification After Foster Care." *Community Alternatives* Vol 5, 2, (Fall).

Margolis, Maxine L. 1984. *Mothers and Such: View of American Women and Why They Change.* Berkeley: University of California Press.

Matas, Robert. 1997. "Foster Parent Hard Job to Fill." *Globe and Mail,* 19 May.

Meyer, Carol H. 1985. "A Feminist Perspective on Foster Family Care: A Redefinition of the Categories." *Child Welfare* Vol LXIV, 3, (May-June).

Meyer, Phillipe. 1977. *The Child and the State.* New York: Cambridge University Press.

Moogk, Peter N. 1982. "Les Petits Sauvages: The Children of Eighteenth-Century New France." In Joy Parr (ed.), *Childhood and Family in Canadian History.* Toronto: McClelland

and Stewart.

Nett, Emily M. 1988. *Canadian Families Past and Present.* Toronto: Butterworth.

Neumann-Clubb, Angela. 1990. *Love in the Blended Family: Falling in Love with a Package Deal.* Toronto: NC Press.

New Brunswick. 1989. *Child Care Services.* Department of Social Services, Fredericton.

———. 1990a. *Foster Home Standards.* Department of Health and Community Service. Fredericton.

———. 1990b. *Report of the Task Force on Foster Homes.* Department of Health and Community Services. Fredericton.

———. 1991. *Playing for Keeps!* Office for Childhood Services. Fredericton.

———. 1992. *Redesign of Foster Home Services in New Brunswick.* Department of Health and Community Services and N.B. Foster Families Association. Fredericton.

———. n.d. Foster Care pamphlet. Department of Health and Community Services. Fredericton.

———. n.d. *Foster Family Manual.* Department of Health and Community Services. Fredericton.

O'Brien, Derek. 1991. *Suffer Little Children.* St. John's: Breakwater.

Oakley, Ann. 1981. "Interviewing Women: A Contradiction in Terms." In H. Roberts (ed.), *Doing Feminist Research.* London: Routledge & Kegan Paul.

Ontario. 1990. *Foster Care as a Residential Family Resource.* Ministry of Community and Social Service. Toronto.

Orenstein, Reuben. 1989. "The New Brunswick Therapeutic Home Program." In Joe Hudson and Burt Galaway (eds.), *Specialist Foster Family Care: A Normalizing Experience.* London: The Haworth Press.

Parsons, Talcott. 1959. "The Social Structure of the Family." In Ruth Nanda Ashen (ed.),*The Family: Its Function and Destiny.* New York: Harper Row.

Pasley, Kay, and Marilyn Ihinger-Tallman. 1987. *Remarriage and Stepparenting.* New York: Guilford Press.

Reddy, Maureen, Martha Roth, and Amy Sheldon (eds). 1994. *Mother Journeys: Feminists Write About Mothering.* Minneapolis: Spinsters Ink.

Rich, Adrienne. 1986. *Of Woman Born*. New York: W.W. Norton.

Rosenberg, Harriet. 1995. "Motherwork, Stress, and Depression: the Cost of Privatized Social Reproduction." In E.D. Nelson and B.W. Robinson (eds.), *Gender in the 1990s: Images, Realities and Issues*. Toronto: Nelson.

Rossiter, Amy. 1988. *From Private to Public*. Toronto: The Women's Press.

Shapiro, Barbara. 1994. "Mothering ... 'without any irritable reaching after fact reason.'" In Maureen T. Reddy, Martha Roth and Amy Sheldon (eds.), *Mother Journeys: Feminists Write about Mothering*. Minneapolis: Spinster Ink.

Shorter, Edward. 1975. *The Making of A Modern Family*. New York: Basic Books.

Smith, Brenda. 1991. "Australian Women and Foster Care: A Feminist Perspective." *Child Welfare* LXX, 2.

Smith, Brenda, and Tina Smith. 1990. "For Love and Money: Women as Foster Mothers." *Affilia* 5, 1, (Spring).

Steinhauer, Paul D. 1991. *The Least Detrimental Alternative*. University of Toronto Press.

Stone, Lawrence. 1977. *The Family, Sex and Marriage*. London: Weidenfield and Nicolson.

Swift, Karen. 1991. "Contradictions in Child Welfare: Neglect and Responsibility." In Carol T. Baines, Patricia M. Evans and Sheila Neysmith (eds.), *Perspectives on Social Welfare*. Toronto: McClelland & Stewart.

———. 1995. *Manufacturing 'Bad Mothers': A Critical Perspective on Child Neglect*. University Press of Toronto.

Synott, Anthony. 1984. "Little Angels, Little Devils: A Sociology of Children." In Alexander Himmelfarb and C. James Richardson (eds.), *Sociology for Canadians*. Toronto: McGraw-Hill Ryerson.

Tilly, Louise A., Joan W. Scott, and Miriam Cohen. 1978. "Women's Work and European Fertility Patterns." In Michael Gordon (ed.), *The American Family in Social-Historical Perspective*. New York: St. Martin's.

Tong, Rosemarie. 1989. *Feminist Thought*. San Francisco: Westview Press.

Ursel, Jane. 1992. *Private Lives, Public Policy*. Toronto: Women's Press.

Walters, Laura Sherman. 1993. *There's a New Family in my House*. Illinois: Harold Shaw.

Waring, Marilyn. 1995. *Sex, Lies and Global Economics* (video). Ottawa: National Film Board.

White, Julie. 1993. *Sisters and Solidarity*. Toronto: Thompson Educational Publishing.

Young, Canon John V. 1964. *History of Children's Aid Society of the County of Saint John*.

Zelizer, Viviana A. Rotman. 1981. *Pricing the Priceless Child*. New York: Basic Books.

Related Titles from Fernwood

Citizens or Consumers?
Social Policy in a Market Society
David Broad (Regina) and Wayne Antony eds.

320pp Paper 1 55266 006 0 $29.95

Social policy is about citizens choosing the kind of society they want to live in. The mid-20th Century Keynesian welfare state can be seen as a citizenship package which included acceptance of intervention by the state to maintain economic growth and social stability, that meant the inclusion of many previously excluded groups in the social policy process and the institutionalization of a collective responsibility for individual welfare. But, with the ascendancy of neo-liberalism, the politics of citizenship is being replaced by a notion of citizens as consumers, whose medium of social interaction and source of economic and social security is the capitalist market.

This book is concerned with social welfare problems and the need for citizen participation in addressing those problems. While all of the authors are critical of the current neo-liberal orthodoxy, none advocates a return to the status quo ante of the post-World War II welfare state. The essays are grouped into three parts: conceptual critiques of neo-liberal social policy; specific empirical analyses of the neo-liberal counter-revolution; and conceptual and practical responses for moving beyond neo-liberalism.

Canada's National Child Benefit
Phoenix or Fizzle?
Douglas Durst (Regina) ed.

110pp Paper 1 55266 009 5 $13.95

The National Child Benefit announced in the 1997 federal Budget promised 850 million dollars to move children out of the welfare rolls and the trap of poverty. This book attempts to outline the key concepts of this new program and set the stage for discussion of its potential impact. The writers do not agree. This book does not present a unified argument either supporting or critiquing the program but raises a series of important issues and concerns regarding the programs effectiveness in addressing child poverty. The question remains: Is this new federal social program a phoenix rising from the ashes of past social welfare programs or just a federal fizzle?

Fetal Alcohol Syndrome /Effect
Developing a Community Response
Jeanette Turpin (Northern B.C.)
and Glen Schmidt (Northern B.C.) eds.

110pp Paper 1 55266 011 7 $13.95

Fetal Alcohol Syndrome and Effects (FAS/E) are particularly serious problems in many northern communities. Canadian material on this subject is lacking and services are poorly developed. Part of the reason has to do with the relatively recent recognition of FAS/E. However there is also the problem of hinterland location and resulting marginalization of populations in Northern parts of the country. The intent of this book is to provide an informative, practical and critical resource that will be useful to people such as social workers, educators, foster parents, case aides and nurses who provide direct service to those affected by FAS/E. The book challenges program planners and policy makers to recognize the seriousness of the problem and its long term effects. Contributors largely represent actual human service workers as opposed to academics.

Blaming Children
Youth Crime, Moral Panics and the Politics of Hate
Bernard Schissel (Saskatchewan)

133pp Paper 1 895686 83 0 $16.95

This book argues that we are on the verge of an acute "moral panic" in this country that, if allowed to continue, will result in the indictment of all adolescents, but especially those that are disadvantaged. Schissel explains the role of the media in this panic—its affiliation with information/political systems, with its readers/viewers, and with corporate Canada. The reality of youth crime is presented in stark contrast to the collective perception that youth crime is expanding at an alarming rate. Schissel discusses the larger structural forces that construct, communicate and perpetuate a belief system that benefits those who have access to power and indicts those who live on the margins of political, social and economic society.

Feminism and Families
Critical Policies and Changing Practices
Meg Luxton ed. (York)

232pp Paper 1 895686 76 8 $23.95

Despite significant changes in family, domestic and interpersonal relations, the prevailing ideology of the heterosexual nuclear family as the norm still shapes social, economic and legal practices. This book argues for feminist debates in all areas affecting families and begins with such important areas as demographics, family law, lesbian parenting, women's friendships, child benefit legislation, and the contradictions of parenting.

Child and Family Policies
Struggles, Strategies and Options
Jane Pulkingham (Simon Fraser)
and Gordon Ternowetsky (Northern BC) eds.

232pp Paper 1 895686 60 1 $22.95

The contributions analyze the implications of government policy shifts showing how they are particularly devastating for children of low-income, welfare, First Nations and single parent families. They suggest policy options and some directions that advocacy groups might take in developing a politics of influence.